AN ENCYCLOPEDIA OF FANTASTIC FACTS

OUR WORLD in NUMBERS

90%

1,380 MILES

300 million

DK

AN ENCYCLOPEDIA OF FANTASTIC FACTS
OUR WORLD in NUMBERS

Written by **CLIVE GIFFORD**

12 in

6 cups

1½ IN

2.6 PINTS

39 trillion

70 MPH

CONTENTS

DK LONDON
Project Editors Kelsie Besaw, Selina Wood
Art Editor Gregory McCarthy
Editors Bharti Bedi, Priyanka Kharbanda, Vicky Richards
Designers Jim Green, Beth Johnston,
Renata Latipova, Anthony Limerick, Lynne Moulding
Picture Researcher Nick Dean, Jo Walton
Managing Editor Francesca Baines
Managing Art Editor Philip Letsu
Production Editor Jacqueline Street-Elkayam
Production Controller Sian Cheung
Senior Jacket Designers Suhita Dharamjit, Akiko Kato
Jacket Designer Tanya Mehrotra
Jackets Design Development Manager Sophia MTT
Senior DTP Designer Harish Aggarwal
Senior Jackets Coordinator Priyanka Sharma-Saddi
Managing Jackets Editor Saloni Singh
Publisher Andrew Mcintyre
Art Director Karen Self
Associate Publishing Director Liz Wheeler
Publishing Director Jonathan Metcalf

First American Edition, 2022
Published in the United States by DK Publishing
1450 Broadway, Suite 801, New York, NY 10018

Copyright © 2022 Dorling Kindersley Limited
DK, a Division of Penguin Random House LLC
22 23 24 25 26 10 9 8 7 6 5 4 3 2 1
001–322075–Apr/2022

A catalog record for this book
is available from the Library of Congress.
ISBN 978-0-7440-2891-1

DK books are available at special discounts when purchased
in bulk for sales promotions, premiums, fund-raising, or
educational use. For details, contact: DK Publishing Special
Markets,
1450 Broadway, Suite 801, New York, NY 10018
SpecialSales@dk.com

Printed and bound in China
For the curious
www.dk.com

This book was made with Forest Stewardship
Council® certified paper – one small step in
DK's commitment to a sustainable future.
For more information go to
www.dk.com/our-green-pledge

NATURE

PEOPLE AND CULTURE

HISTORY

SCIENCE AND TECHNOLOGY

NOTE: THE FACTS AND STATISTICS IN THIS BOOK WERE CORRECT AT THE TIME OF GOING TO PRESS.

A WORLD OF NUMBERS

It's impossible to imagine our lives without numbers. The first counting systems were invented thousands of years ago, and today we use many different types of numbers to help us understand the world around us. Throughout this book, you'll discover hundreds of amazing number facts that answer questions like the ones below and many more.

How **LONG AGO** was the Roman Empire?

We use time to measure history, as well as to keep track of the seconds, minutes, and hours in a day or the days and months in a year. Without time, we wouldn't be able to count our age or get to school on time.

How **MANY** stars are there?

Counting can add up almost anything—from people and pets to stars and sea creatures—and helps us to think about really big numbers and concepts.

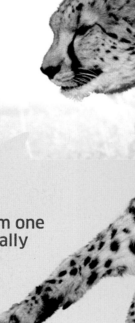

How **FAST** is a cheetah?

Speed is the time it takes to travel from one point to another. Some things move really fast, such as cheetahs and racecars, while other things move slowly, such as glaciers and snails.

How **WIDE** is the Grand Canyon?

Measurements for short distances, such as inches and feet, tell us how wide or long something is, while long distances, such as miles, tell us how far we'd have to travel to get from one country to another.

How **MUCH** does a film cost to make?

Numbers used for money can show the value of things, from the price of popcorn or movie tickets to the budgets needed to make big blockbuster films.

What **PERCENTAGE** of the world's population speaks Chinese?

When we use percentages, we're describing a part of something out of a whole. It helps us understand things like how many people out of the entire world population speak a language.

How **TALL** is the Burj Khalifa?

Measuring height tells us how tall something is, from the tallest skyscrapers to the loftiest mountain peaks. Height can even help mark the passage of time, as you measure how much you grow every year.

SPACE

mysterious UNIVERSE

From the tiniest atomic particle to the largest galaxy, the universe is everything that exists. It was formed billions of years ago in a massive explosion known as the Big Bang. The universe is so big that it takes light billions of years to travel across it.

The universe is approximately

13.8 BILLION YEARS OLD.

18 BILLION °F

(10 billion °C) was the temperature of the universe **1 SECOND** after **THE BIG BANG.**

The **FIRST ATOMS** didn't form until

380,000

YEARS after the Big Bang.

STARS ARE BORN in clouds of dust and gas, called **NEBULAE.** Collections of stars bound together by gravity form **GALAXIES.** IC 1101, one of the largest-known galaxies, contains around **100 trillion stars.**

THE EAGLE NEBULA is 7,000 **LIGHT-YEARS** away from Earth.

The **UNIVERSE** was about **9 BILLION YEARS OLD** when our **SOLAR SYSTEM** first began to form.

The **FIRST IMAGE** of a **BLACK HOLE** was captured in **2019.**

Around **TWO-THIRDS** of all known galaxies are **SPIRAL-SHAPED.**

ONLY 5% **OF THE UNIVERSE IS VISIBLE TO US.** The remaining **95%** is made up of invisible **DARK MATTER** and mysterious **DARK ENERGY.**

A **LIGHT-YEAR** is the distance a beam of light travels in **1 EARTH YEAR,** and is equal to **5.9 TRILLION MILES** (9.5 trillion km).

A **YEAR** is the time it takes **EARTH** to make **1 full orbit** around the **SUN.** Earth's year lasts for **365.26 days.** The **SHORTEST-KNOWN YEAR** on an exoplanet is **28 MINUTES.**

Exoplanets are planets that exist **OUTSIDE OF OUR SOLAR SYSTEM.** By September 2021, NASA had confirmed the total number of exoplanets at **4,521.**

Our **SOLAR SYSTEM** lies about **25,800 LIGHT-YEARS** away from the **CENTER** of the **MILKY WAY.**

In **1924,** US astronomer **EDWIN HUBBLE** confirmed the **Andromeda nebula** as the **FIRST-KNOWN GALAXY** other than the Milky Way.

One of the **SMALLEST GALAXIES** ever observed, **Segue 2,** is home to as few as **1,000 STARS.**

The **ANDROMEDA** and **MILKY WAY** galaxies are expected to **COLLIDE** in **4.5 billion years.**

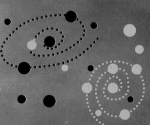

Spectacular STARS

Stars are giant balls of burning hot gas, held together by gravity, that are born and die over billions of years. The biggest stars die in massive explosions called supernovas and then collapse to form incredibly dense neutron stars. The Sun is a star in the Milky Way galaxy.

99.8% of all the **MASS** in our **SOLAR SYSTEM** is contained in the **SUN.**

At approximately **4.6 BILLION YEARS OLD,** the **SUN** is roughly **HALFWAY** through its life.

It takes more than **8 minutes** for the **LIGHT FROM THE SUN** to reach Earth.

88 CONSTELLATIONS (groups of visible stars) are approved by the **INTERNATIONAL ASTRONOMICAL UNION.**

The **BRIGHTEST STAR** in the night sky is **SIRIUS,** the **DOG STAR.** It has a surface temperature of **17,440°F** (9,670°C).

The **OLDEST STARS** are about **12 billion years old.**

36 constellations feature **ANIMALS,** including a lion, a bear, a scorpion, and **4 DOGS.**

Canadian **KATHRYN AURORA GRAY** was just **10 years old** when she discovered a **SUPERNOVA** in the Camelopardalis constellation in **2011.**

On a **CLEAR NIGHT,** it is possible to see **2,500—5,000** stars from Earth with an unaided eye.

1,300,000

EARTHS can fit inside the **SUN**.

A **TABLESPOON** of a **NEUTRON STAR** would weigh

2,000 BILLION LB
(900 billion kg), the weight of

150
Great Pyramids
from ancient Egypt.

In 1054 CE, a **SUPERNOVA EXPLODING 6,500 light-years** away from Earth **COULD BE SEEN DURING DAYTIME** for **23 DAYS**.

It would take a **JET AIRLINER**

4.8 MILLION YEARS
to travel to **PROXIMA CENTAURI**, the second-nearest star to Earth, **4.24 light-years away.**

The Milky Way is made up of 100–400 BILLION STARS.

The **SURFACE TEMPERATURE** of the **COOLEST-KNOWN STAR**, the brown dwarf **WISE 1828+2650**, is

127°F
(52°C)–barely hotter than a **cup of tea.**

It takes the **SUN** at least

220 million years
to make **1 ORBIT** of our galaxy.

91%
of the **ATOMS** that make up the **SUN** are **HYDROGEN**, the lightest of all chemical elements.

27,000,000°F
(15,000,000°C) is the estimated temperature of **THE SUN'S CORE.**

The **FASTEST-KNOWN PULSAR** (a spinning neutron star)–**PSR J1748–2446AD**–makes

716 spins per second.

There are an estimated

100 BILLION TRILLION
STARS in the Universe.

Earth's
moon

Reflecting light from the Sun to glow in the night sky, the Moon is our closest neighbor in space. Its bleak yet beautiful landscape is marked by rubble, craters, and dusty plains.

The **MOON** is around **238,850 MILES** (384,400 km) **FROM EARTH**—it takes just over **60 hours** to travel there.

2 GOLF BALLS were hit on the Moon by **Apollo 14** astronaut **ALAN SHEPARD.**

The **DIAMETER** of **SOUTH POLE-AITKEN BASIN**—the largest and oldest-known crater on the Moon—is **1,553 MILES** (2,500 km).

In **1969,** Apollo 11 astronauts **Neil Armstrong** and **Buzz Aldrin** became the first humans to set foot on the Moon.

The Moon takes **27.3 DAYS** to **ORBIT EARTH** and rotate on its axis.

12 humans walked on the **MOON** during **6 Apollo missions** (1969–1972).

7.5 minutes is the maximum length of time of a total **SOLAR ECLIPSE**, when the Moon **BLOCKS OUT** the whole disc of the Sun.

TEMPERATURES on the **MOON** range from **–280°F** (–173°C) to **261°F** (127°C).

49 MOONS could fit inside Earth.

5,185 CRATERS ON THE MOON have a diameter of **12.5 MILES** (20 km) or more.

Astronomers think the Moon **FORMED** from debris after a **COLLISION** between Earth and another Mars-sized planet around **4.5 BILLION YEARS AGO.**

The Moon's gravity is just **17%** of gravity on Earth.

They brought back to Earth **842 LB** (382 km) of **MOON ROCKS.**

In **1959**, the **FAR SIDE** of the Moon—the side that is always facing away from Earth—was **FIRST PHOTOGRAPHED**, by Soviet spacecraft **LUNA 3.**

The **DIAMETER OF THE MOON** is **2,160 MILES** (3,475 km)–less than the **WIDTH OF THE US.**

26 MILES (42 km) is the distance that the Soviet rover **LUNOKHOD 2** roamed on the Moon in **1973.**

The **MOON** is **MOVING AWAY** from Earth at a rate of **1.48 IN** (3.78 cm) per year.

The PLANETS

Earth is not the only planet orbiting the Sun. Another seven planets and five dwarf planets, along with many moons and numerous asteroids, travel around the Sun, making up the solar system.

VALLES MARINERIS, a system of canyons on Mars, is **5 times LONGER** and almost **4 times DEEPER** than the Grand Canyon.

WINDS ON NEPTUNE can race at up to **1,300 MPH** (2,100 km/h)– the **FASTEST** in the solar system.

1,300 EARTHS would **FIT INSIDE JUPITER,** which is almost **TWICE** as massive as all the other planets put together.

SATURN has more than **80 moons. TITAN,** its largest moon, is even bigger than the planet **MERCURY.**

In **1781, URANUS** became the **FIRST PLANET** to be discovered **USING A TELESCOPE.**

A DAY AND NIGHT on Mercury last **176 EARTH DAYS.**

Neptune is **30 times** farther **away from the Sun** than Earth.

If you weighed **110 LB** (50 kg) on Earth, your **weight on Jupiter** would be **278 LB** (126.4 kg).

OLYMPUS MONS volcano on Mars is **16 MILES** (25 km) high—almost **3 TIMES** the height of **MOUNT EVEREST.**

MAAT MONS, with a diameter of **245 MILES** (395 km), is the **LARGEST** of more than **1,600 volcanoes** on **VENUS.**

Following its discovery in 1930, **PLUTO** was considered a planet for **76 YEARS.** In 2006, it was **RECLASSIFIED AS A DWARF PLANET.**

SATURN'S BRIGHT RINGS are about **174,000 MILES** (280,000 km) wide and only around **330 FT** (100 m) thick.

MERCURY has an **IRON CORE** that makes up about **61%** of the planet's volume.

More than **1,100,000** small chunks of rock and metal, known as **ASTEROIDS,** orbit the **SUN** in the **ASTEROID BELT.**

PLUTO'S name was suggested by Venetia Burney, an **11-YEAR-OLD ENGLISH SCHOOLGIRL,** in 1930. She received a **£5 note** as a reward.

EXPLORING SPACE

From walking on the Moon to sending probes beyond the solar system, scientists are always pushing the boundaries of the final frontier.

The **FIRST HUMAN SPACEFLIGHT,** by Russian astronaut **YURI GAGARIN** in 1961, lasted just **108 MINUTES.**

45 minutes
is the time it takes to **PUT ON A SPACESUIT,** including the special clothes worn underneath to **keep the astronaut cool.**

NASA's **SPACE SHUTTLE PROGRAM** operated for

30 years,
from **1981** to **2011.**

CHINA'S FIRST HUMAN SPACEFLIGHT in 2003 saw Yang Liwei, chosen from more than **1,500 CANDIDATES,** orbit Earth

14 times
aboard Shenzhou 5.

NASA uses a collection of **GIANT RADIO ANTENNAS** called the **DEEP SPACE NETWORK** (DSN), across **3 DIFFERENT SITES,** which can track a spacecraft

BILLIONS
of miles from Earth.

The Gaia space observatory can **MEASURE** objects in space **400,000 TIMES FAINTER** than the eye can see.

248,655 MILES (400,171 km) was the distance **3 ASTRONAUTS** on the **APOLLO 13** mission traveled from Earth—the **FARTHEST** anyone has ventured.

The **NEW SHEPARD 4** spacecraft launched a test flight in **2021**, which carried both the **YOUNGEST ASTRONAUT, AGED 18,** and the **OLDEST, AGED 90,** into space.

In 1984, **4 astronauts** used a Manned Maneuvering Unit (MMU) **JET PACK** to float **300 FT** (90 m) from their spacecraft and retrieve **2 SATELLITES.**

Spoken greetings in **55 LANGUAGES** plus **115 IMAGES** of Earth are stored on a gold-plated disc aboard the **VOYAGER SPACE PROBES** in case they encounter extraterrestrial life.

On Earth, the **MMU JET PACK** and **SPACESUIT** weighed around **585 LB** (266 kg)

The **Voyager 1 space probe** was launched in **1977** and is now more than **14 BILLION MILES** (23.5 billion km) away from Earth.

56 MILES (90 km) is the total distance traveled on the **MOON** by **all 3 LUNAR ROVING VEHICLES** (LRV). The LRV had a top speed of **11.2 MPH** (18 km/h).

THE COMBINED DISTANCE
flown by the **5 NASA SPACE SHUTTLES** in their 135 missions was **513,700,000 MILES** (826,700,000 km).

Russian cosmonaut **ANATOLY SOLOVYEV** has made a record **16** spacewalks totaling **82 hours, 22 minutes.**

CHRISTINA KOCH holds the record for the **LONGEST SPACEFLIGHT BY A WOMAN.** She spent **328 DAYS IN SPACE.**

THE JUNO SPACE PROBE carried **3 aluminum LEGO FIGURES** to Jupiter.

TOP 10
LARGEST LAUNCHERS

1
SATURN V • US • 354 FT (111 m)
Active years: **1967–1973**

Saturn V is not only the largest but also the heaviest launch vehicle. Fully fueled, it weighed 6.2 million lb (2.8 million kg)–more than the weight of 450 male African savanna elephants.

2
N1 • Soviet Union; test launcher • **244 FT** (105 m)
Active years: **1969–1972**

The large N1 launcher was originally built to take astronauts to the Moon but was never successfully launched.

3
ARES I-X • US; test launcher • **309 FT** (94.2 m)
Active year: **2009**

Ares I-X was a NASA prototype and was only launched once, completing a brief test flight.

4
DELTA IV HEAVY • US • 236 FT (72 m)
Active years: **2004–PRESENT**

Able to carry 34-ton loads into Earth's orbit, the Delta IV uses two additional rocket boosters to get itself into space.

5
SPACEX FALCON HEAVY • US • 230 FT (70 m)
Active years: **2018–PRESENT**

Falcon Heavy is the most powerful rocket operational today. Its 27 engines can generate 5 million pounds of thrust.

6
SPACEX FALCON 9 • US • 230 FT (70 m)
Active years: **2010–PRESENT**

A reusable rocket, Falcon 9 was designed to carry people or objects into space at cheaper cost.

7
ANGARA-A5 • Russia • **210 FT** (64 m)
Active years: **2014–PRESENT**

The Angara-A5 was commissioned by the Russian government and uses a less toxic fuel than its predecessor, the Proton-M.

8
DELTA IV • US • 205 FT (62.5 m)
Active years: **2002–PRESENT**

Along with other Delta models, the Delta IV carries the largest existing hydrogen-burning engine.

9
CHANG ZHENG 2F (Long March Rocket) • China • **203 FT** (62 m)
Active years: **1999–PRESENT**

The Chang Zheng 2F is a two-stage rocket with four boosters, designed to launch crewed spacecraft.

10
ARIANE 4 • European Space Agency; ESA • **192 FT 8 IN** (58.72 m)
Active years: **1990–2003**

During its working life, Ariane 4 made 113 successful launches, carrying many satellites into space.

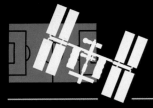

The ISS is **357 FT** (109 m) **WIDE**, which is about the same length as a **SOCCER FIELD**.

Traveling at **17,100 MPH** (27,500 km/h), ISS orbits Earth about **16 times** in a day.

With a total of more than **879 DAYS** over **5 MISSIONS**, cosmonaut Gennady Padalka holds the record for the **MOST TIME SPENT IN SPACE**.

Without gravity, astronauts' spines **RELAX**, and they can grow up to **3 IN** (7.6 cm) **TALLER** while they live in space.

The first space tourist, American **DENNIS TITO**, reportedly paid **$20,000,000** to fly to the ISS in 1991.

The first **ALL-FEMALE SPACEWALK**, performed by US astronauts Jessica Meir and Christina Koch in 2019, lasted **7 HOURS AND 17 MINUTES**.

In **2007**, astronaut Sunita Williams ran **4 hours, 24 minutes** on the ISS treadmill and became the first person to run a **MARATHON IN SPACE**.

During **SPACEWALKS**, astronauts wear an **UNDERGARMENT** that **PUMPS WATER** through **300 FT** (91.5 m) of **NARROW TUBES** to regulate their temperature.

In **1982**, the Salyut 7 space station crew grew the **FIRST PLANTS** that flowered and produced seeds **IN SPACE**.

The cupola of the ISS has **7 windows** that face Earth—**6 SIDE WINDOWS** and **1 AT THE TOP**.

An Australian town issued NASA with a **$400 FINE** for **LITTERING** after **DEBRIS** from US space station **SKYLAB** fell on it in 1979.

The first space station was **SALYUT 1**, launched by Russia in 1971. It travelled **73.7 MILLION MILES** (118.6 million km) during its **175** days in orbit.

LIVING IN SPACE

Space stations are giant orbiting spacecraft that allow astronauts to live and work in space. Since the 1970s, many space stations have been built by the US, Russia, and China, but only two are orbiting Earth today, including the International Space Station (ISS).

Up to **8** **SPACECRAFT** can be docked to the **ISS** at the same time.

To date, **242** **ASTRONAUTS** from **19 NATIONS** have visited the **ISS.**

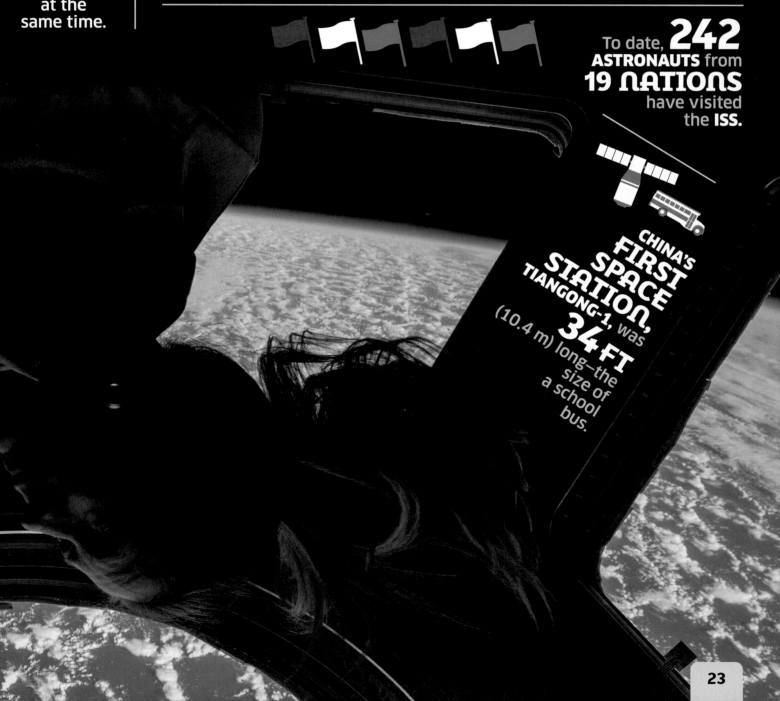

CHINA'S FIRST SPACE STATION, TIANGONG-1, was **34 FT** (10.4 m) long—the size of a school bus.

EARTH

Earth **ORBITS** the Sun at an average **DISTANCE** of

92,956,050 MILES
(149,598,262 km). Driving that distance at **50 MPH** (80 km/h) would take more than

213 YEARS.

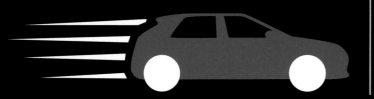

Just **4 ELEMENTS**—iron, oxygen, silicon, and magnesium—make up

90%
of **EARTH'S MASS.**

EARTH was formed around

4.54
BILLION YEARS AGO.

The **INNER CORE** of Earth is about the same temperature as the **SURFACE OF THE SUN**— **9,932°F** (5,500°C).

Earth has a slight bulge in the middle. The **CIRCUMFERENCE** around its **EQUATOR** is **24,900 MILES** (40,075 km), about **42 MILES** (67 km) longer than around its **POLES.**

The mass of Earth is

9 TIMES
that of

MARS.

31%
of **EARTH'S LAND** is covered in **FORESTS.**

Earth is the **5TH-LARGEST PLANET IN THE SOLAR SYSTEM,** with an average diameter of

7,918 MILES
(12,742 km).

Earth's rocky **MANTLE** is around

1,802 MILES
(2,900 km) thick and makes up **TWO-THIRDS** of Earth's mass.

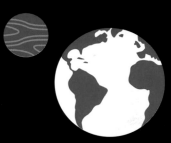

Our planet has **4 LAYERS:** the inner and outer cores, a rocky mantle, and the surface crust.

A **WATER MOLECULE** spends about **10 DAYS** in the **ATMOSPHERE** before it returns to Earth as rain, sleet, dew, or snow.

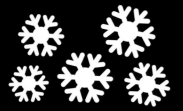

90% of the **MOISTURE** in the atmosphere is caused by **WATER EVAPORATING** from Earth's surface.

The BLUE PLANET

Our astonishing planet looks like a swirling blue marble from space. Life has been able to flourish on Earth due to its size, its distance from the Sun, the presence of water on its surface, and its thick, oxygen-rich atmosphere.

Without the **ATMOSPHERE** to **TRAP HEAT,** Earth's average temperature would be **59°F** (33°C) **COLDER** than today.

Earth's rocky surface is **BROKEN UP** into large slabs called **TECTONIC PLATES.** There are **7 MAJOR** plates and many smaller ones.

¾–2¾ IN (2–7 cm) is the **RATE** at which **TECTONIC PLATES MOVE** each year—about the rate at which your fingernails grow.

68.7% of Earth's **FRESH WATER** is locked in **ICE CAPS AND GLACIERS.**

Earth is tilted **23.5°** on its side, which gives us the **DIFFERING SEASONS** in the northern and southern hemispheres (halves of the planet).

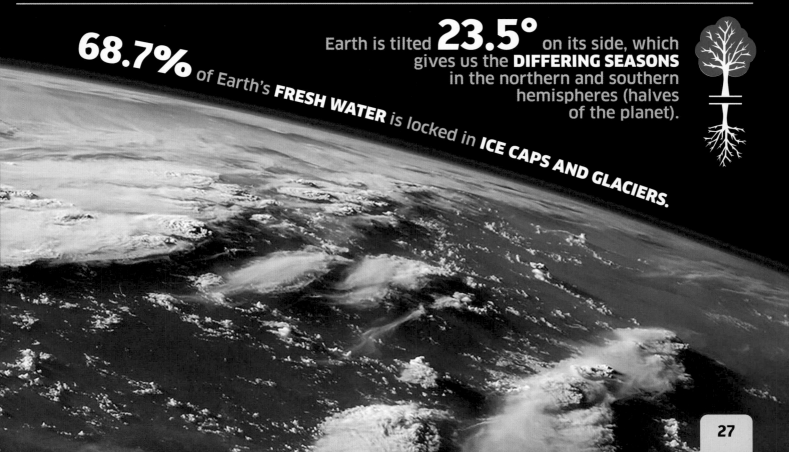

There are **3 TYPES OF ROCK:** sedimentary, igneous, and metamorphic.

A glass tube called a **FULGURITE** is formed when a **LIGHTNING BOLT** with a minimum temperature of **3,270°F** (1,800°C) strikes sand or rock.

About **80—90% OF ROCKS** on Earth's surface are **SEDIMENTARY** rocks.

BLUE DIAMONDS comprise only **0.02%** of all diamonds. They form at depths of at least **410 MILES** (660 km)—**4 TIMES DEEPER** than regular diamonds.

In Death Valley National Park large rocks called **SAILING STONES** can weigh up to **660 LB** (300 kg) and have been moved as much as **1,600 FT** (500 m) by wind and ice.

Made from **SILICON** and **OXYGEN**, **25%** of all known **minerals** are **silicates** and make up about **90%** of **EARTH'S CRUST.**

LIMESTONE STALACTITES— mineral deposits hanging from cave ceilings—grow an average of **4 IN** (10 cm) **EVERY 1,000 YEARS.**

GIANT'S CAUSEWAY is a **50- TO 60-MILLION-YEAR-OLD** area in Northern Ireland that contains roughly **40,000 BASALT ROCK COLUMNS.**

EROSION of **LIMESTONE ROCKS** has formed more than **120 caves** at New Mexico's Carlsbad Caverns. One of the caves, **LECHUGUILLA,** is more than **138 miles** (223 km) long.

ROCKS AND GEMSTONES

Rocks form Earth's crust and are made up of more than 3,000 different minerals. Gemstones are minerals that can be cut and polished and are valued for their beauty and rarity.

Diamonds
are formed under intense heat and pressure at **DEPTHS OF** **87–118 miles** (140–190 km) below the surface of Earth.

The **GRANITE QUARRY** at Mount Airy, NC, is spread across about **60 ACRES** (24 hectares)—an area equal to **66 FOOTBALL FIELDS.**

The first working **LASER** was constructed in **1960** using a **RUBY GEMSTONE.**

Each year, more than **176 MILLION TONS** of the rock **BAUXITE** is mined, which is then processed to obtain **ALUMINUM.**

About **6 FT 6 IN** (2 m) long, the **GAVAL DASH** stone in Azerbaijan makes a sound **LIKE A TAMBOURINE** when struck.

Only **20** people per day are allowed to **VISIT** the **WAVE** sandstone rock formation in Arizona. In 2019, more than **200,000** people applied for **PERMITS.**

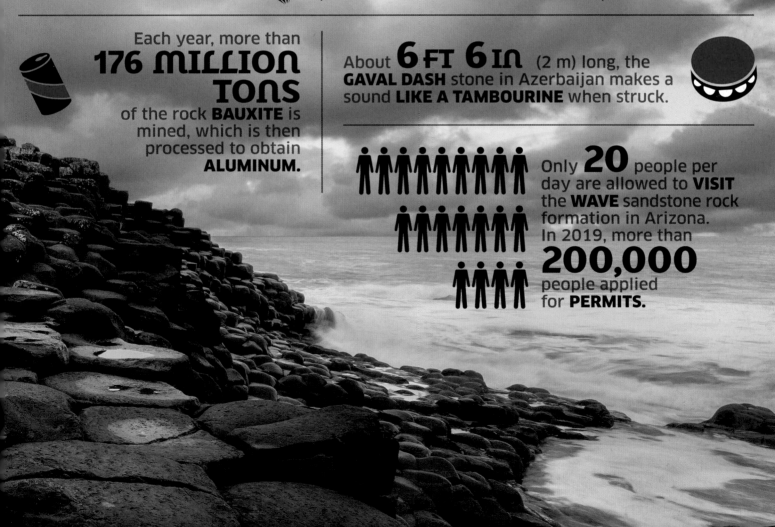

TOP 10 TALLEST MOUNTAINS

MOUNT EVEREST • China, Nepal
29,029 FT (8,848 m) • Peak first climbed **1953**

Located in the Himalayas, Mount Everest is the highest point on Earth. The movement of tectonic plates means it is still "growing" by about 2 in (5 cm) per year.

1

2 **K2** • China, Pakistan • **28,251 FT** (8,611 m)
Peak first climbed **1954**

K2 sits in the Karakoram mountain range, home to the greatest concentration of high mountains in the world.

3 **KANGCHENJUNGA** • India, Nepal • **26,169 FT** (8,586 m)
Peak first climbed **1955**

Kangchenjunga was thought to be the world's tallest mountain until 1852, when new calculations were made.

4 **LHOTSE** • China, Nepal • **27,940 FT** (8,516 m)
Peak first climbed **1956**

On Lhotse's western side lies Lhotse Face—a wall of hard ice that climbers must pass to reach Everest.

5 **MAKALU** • China, Nepal • **27,838 FT** (8,485 m)
Peak first climbed **1955**

Pyramid-shaped Makalu has many exposed ridges, making it one of the hardest mountains to climb.

6 **CHO OYU** • China, Nepal • **26,864 FT** (8,188 m)
Peak first climbed **1954**

In the Himalayas, Cho Oyu lies near the key mountain pass and trade route of Nangpa La.

7 **DHAULAGIRI I** • Nepal • **26,795 FT** (8,167 m)
Peak first climbed **1960**

The high peak Dhaulagiri I is surrounded by the tributaries of major rivers, including the Bheri and the Kali Gandaki.

8 **MANASLU** • Nepal • **26,781 FT** (8,163 m)
Peak first climbed **1956**

Endangered animals such as snow leopards and red pandas live around Manaslu's valleys, a protected conservation area.

9 **NANGA PARBAT** • Pakistan • **26,660 FT** (8,126 m)
Peak first climbed **1953**

The south of Nanga Parbat features the 15,000-ft (4,500-m) Rupal Face, considered the highest mountain face in the world.

0 **ANNAPURNA I** • Nepal • **26,545 FT** (8,091 m)
Peak first climbed **1950**

Rocky peak Annapurna I was the first mountain of more than 26,000 ft (8,000 m) to be climbed.

Earthquakes and
VOLCANOES

Earth's crust is made up of many pieces called tectonic plates, which slowly move around on the hot molten rock underneath. Earthquakes occur when two plates slide past each other, producing shock waves. Volcanoes are formed when hot molten rock is forced up to the surface through cracks in the crust.

When measured from its base on the seafloor, **HAWAII'S MAUNA LOA** has a total height of **56,332 FT** (17,170 m), making it the world's **TALLEST** VOLCANO.

66,000,000 TONS of sulfur were sent up into the atmosphere by the **1815** eruption of **MOUNT TAMBORA.**

In **1935,** Charles F. Richter introduced the **RICHTER SCALE** to measure **EARTHQUAKE MAGNITUDE** on a scale from **1 to 10.**

EVERY YEAR, there are about **500,000** detectable earthquakes. About **100,000** can be felt, and only around **100** cause damage.

The temperature of **LAVA**–hot molten rock emitted from a volcano–is around 1,300–2,200°F (700–1,200°C).

The **FASTEST SHOCK WAVES** from an earthquake can travel through the ground at speeds of **11,200—17,900 MPH** (18,000–28,800 km/h).

Located in the **ANDES MOUNTAINS** in South America at **22,614 FT** (6,893 m), **OJOS DEL SALADO** is the world's **HIGHEST ACTIVE VOLCANO.**

In **79 CE,** Mount Vesuvius **ERUPTED AND BURIED** the ancient Roman cities of **POMPEII AND HERCULANEUM.**

ALASKA experiences a **MAGNITUDE 7** earthquake almost every year and a **MAGNITUDE 8 OR HIGHER** once every **14 YEARS.**

There are about **1,500 ACTIVE VOLCANOES** in the world.

In February 2010, an **8.8-MAGNITUDE** earthquake in Chile **MOVED THE CITY** of Concepción about **10 FT** (3.05 m) to the west.

The **volcanic eruption** of **Krakatoa, Indonesia,** in 1883 was heard more than **1,900 MILES** (3,000 km) away, and the **ASHES** rose about **50 MILES** (80 km) up into the atmosphere.

A **9.5-MAGNITUDE** earthquake in **VALDIVIA, CHILE,** in 1960 is the **strongest quake ever recorded.** It left about **2,000,000** people homeless.

90% of earthquakes and **75% of volcanoes** in the world occur along the **"RING OF FIRE,"** the belt of territory surrounding the Pacific Ocean.

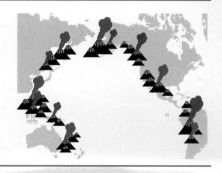

40 MPH (60 km/h) is the speed at which lava flowed from Mount Nyiragongo, Congo, in 1977–the **fastest lava flow** ever recorded.

107,000 estimated **FLIGHTS WERE CANCELED** due to the volcanic ash ejected during the **eruption of Eyjafjallajökull,** Iceland, in 2010.

PARÍCUTIN volcano emerged in the middle of a Mexican farmer's **CORNFIELD IN 1943** and grew **1,102 FT** (336 m) **TALL** in about a year.

Natural
WONDERS

From the top of the tallest mountains to the bottom of the deepest caves, our unique planet is made up of amazing landscapes and extraordinary wildlife.

Every year on **CHRISTMAS ISLAND** in **AUSTRALIA,** at least **40 million RED CRABS** migrate from the forests to the ocean to **REPRODUCE,** with **1-2 CRABS CROWDING 10-SQ-FT** (1-sq-m) area of beach in some places.

Covering an area of **4,086 SQ MILES** (10,582 sq km), **SALAR DE UYUNI** in Bolivia is the world's **LARGEST SALT FLAT,** containing about **11 BILLION tons of salt.**

WULINGYUAN in China has more than **3,000 SANDSTONE PILLARS AND PEAKS,** formed by water erosion of the **380-million-year-old** sandstone.

New Zealand's **WAITOMO CAVES** are lit up by **HUNDREDS OF THOUSANDS OF GLOWWORMS** that dangle sticky threads up to **20 IN** (50 cm) **LONG** from walls and ceilings to trap prey.

The world's **LARGEST BEAVER DAM,** measuring **2,788 FT** (850 m) long, was discovered in Alberta, Canada, in **2007.**

Old Faithful geyser at Yellowstone Park, erupts about **20 times a day.** Each eruption expels **3,700—8,400 GALLONS** (14,000–31,800 liters) of water.

Every second, **740,000 GALLONS** (2.8 million liters) of **WATER** flow over the **3 FALLS** that compose **NIAGARA FALLS.**

Made up of rocks up to **2 BILLION YEARS OLD,** the **GRAND CANYON** in Arizona, US, is **1 MILE** (1.6 km) **DEEP** and **227 MILES** (446 km) **LONG.**

At **1,142 FT** (348 m), **ULURU** in Australia is the world's **LARGEST ROCK.** At its highest point, it is **TALLER THAN THE EIFFEL TOWER.**

Discovered in **2009,** the **400-FT-** (122-m-) long **XIANREN BRIDGE** over China's Buliu River is the world's **LONGEST NATURAL ARCH.**

Mexico's **CAVE OF CRYSTALS** contains crystals measuring up to **36 FT** (11 m) **LONG** and weighing up to **55 tons.**

Water drops **3,212 FT** (979 m) from Venezuela's **Angel Falls,** the highest falls in the world.

There are more than **2,000** named **ROCK ARCHES** in the **ARCHES NATIONAL PARK,** in Utah.

Puerto Princesa is a **5-MILE-** (8.2-km-) **LONG** navigable **underground river** that runs beneath the Philippines' St. Paul mountain range.

Trees and
FORESTS

There are more than 60,000 species of tree, ranging from tiny species no bigger than your hand to sequoias the size of skyscrapers. As well as providing timber, trees and forests reduce soil erosion, absorb carbon dioxide, and enrich the environment.

JUST 3 COUNTRIES—Russia, Brazil, and Canada—are home to
40.8% of the world's forests.

46,000 SQ. MILES (119,000 sq km) of tree cover were **LOST TO LOGGING AND FIRES** during 2019—an area **ALMOST 3 TIMES** THE SIZE OF SWITZERLAND.

The **TALLEST TREE SPECIES**—the coast redwood—can grow to a **HEIGHT** of
380 FT
(116 m).

RAINFORESTS cover just **6%** of land on Earth, but are home to **MORE THAN HALF** of all **ANIMAL AND PLANT SPECIES.**

A SINGLE MATURE OAK TREE
can provide a home for
500 SPECIES
of birds, insects, fungi, and lichens.

BAOBABS are **Africa's oldest trees,** known to live up to **3,000 years.**

The Coulter pine produces **GIANT CONES** that weigh up to **8 LB** (3.6 kg)—as much as a **NEWBORN BABY.**

In **2016,** **A REFORESTATION PROGRAM** in Uttar Pradesh, India, saw **800,000 PEOPLE** plant
50,414,058
TREES IN 24 HOURS.

The **LEAVES** of the **RAFFIA PALM TREE** *Raphia regalis* can grow up to **82 FT** (25 m) long— **5 FT** (1.5 m) longer than a tennis court.

A BIRCH TREE can produce **1 million** seeds in a year.

A **SOCCER-FIELD-SIZED AREA** of tropical rainforest **WAS LOST EVERY 6 SECONDS** during 2019.

Globally, the **NUMBER OF TREES** has been **REDUCED BY 46%** since human civilization began around **12,000 YEARS AGO.**

The **EXPLOSIVE FRUIT PODS** of the sandbox tree **HURL SEEDS AWAY** at speeds of up to **157 MPH** (252 km/h). The seeds can travel **328 FT** (100 m).

DWARF WILLOW TREES grow to a maximum height of just **2³/8 IN** (6 cm).

BATS pollinate the **8-IN-** (20-cm-) **WIDE FLOWERS** of the **BAOBAB TREE.**

4,853 YEARS is the **ESTIMATED AGE** in 2021 of Methuselah, a **GREAT BASIN BRISTLECONE PINE,** whose precise location in California's Inyo National Forest is **kept secret.**

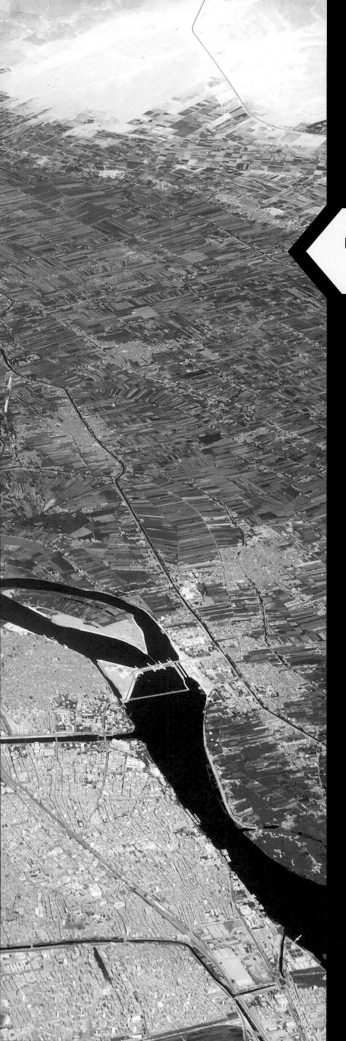

TOP 10
LONGEST RIVERS

1 **NILE** • Africa • **4,132 MILES** (6,650 km)
Outflow: Mediterranean Sea

Throughout history, the Nile River has been a crucial resource for agriculture and fishing in northeastern Africa. It flows north through 11 countries before emptying into the Mediterranean Sea.

2 **AMAZON–UCAYALI–APURÍMAC** • South America
3,976 MILES (6,500 km) • Outflow: Atlantic Ocean

The largest and widest river, the Amazon carries one-fifth of all the fresh water entering the world's oceans.

3 **YANGTZE** • Asia • **3,915 MILES** (6,300 km)
Outflow: East China Sea

The Yangtze is the longest river to flow through just one country (China), passing through more than 30 cities.

4 **MISSISSIPPI–MISSOURI–RED ROCK** • North America
5,971 KM (3,710 miles) • Outflow: Gulf of Mexico

Beginning as a 10-ft- (3-m-) wide stream in Minnesota, the Mississippi flows through 10 US states.

5 **YENISEY–BAIKAL–SELENGA** • Asia
3,442 MILES (5,540 km) • Outflow: Kara Sea

In Russia, the Yenisey flows through Lake Baikal—the world's largest freshwater lake.

6 **HUANG HE** (Yellow) • Asia
3,395 MILES (5,464 km) • Outflow: Yellow Sea

Huang He is called the Yellow River due to the 1.76 billion tons of muddy silt it carries every year.

7 **OB–IRTYSH** • Asia • **3,362 MILES** (5,410 km)
Outflow: Arctic Ocean

For more than half the year, the Ob-Irtysh river system, found in western Siberia, is frozen over and impassable.

8 **PARANÁ** • South America
3,032 MILES (4,880 km) • Outflow: Atlantic Ocean

Sitting on the Paraná is the Itaipú Dam—the second-largest hydroelectric power station in the world.

9 **CONGO** • Africa • **2,920 MILES** (4,700 km)
Outflow: Atlantic Ocean

The capitals of the Republic of the Congo and the Democratic Republic of the Congo lie on either side of this river.

10 **AMUR–ARGUN** • Asia • **2,761 MILES** (4,444 km)
Outflow: Sea of Okhotsk

The Amur River is home to more than 120 unique fish species, including the predatory kaluga.

Oceans and
SEAS

Containing a staggering 97 percent of all the world's water, the oceans form an interconnected watery world that covers approximately 71 percent of our planet's surface. Oceans are where life began around 3.5 billion years ago.

Oceans absorb around **30%** of the **CARBON DIOXIDE EMISSIONS** produced by **HUMANS.**

Almost **3.5%** of the weight of **SEAWATER** comes from **DISSOLVED SALTS.**

Coral reefs
cover less than **1%** of the **OCEAN FLOOR**, yet they support about **25%** of all **MARINE LIFE.**

As many as
3 MILLION
SHIPWRECKS
rest on **OCEAN FLOORS** around the world.

More than **80%** of the oceans are yet to be **fully explored** and **mapped.**

12,080 FT (3,682 m) is the estimated **AVERAGE DEPTH** of the world's oceans.

The **OCEANS** produce more than **50%** of all the **WORLD'S OXYGEN.**

The first **CORAL REEFS** appeared about **500 million years ago.**

TSUNAMI WAVES

travel at **310–620 MPH** (500–1,000 km/h) in deep ocean water, **SLOWING DOWN** but **GROWING IN HEIGHT** as they near land.

The largest seaweed, *MACROCYSTIS PYRIFERA* **(GIANT KELP),** can reach heights of more than **100 FT** (30 m) and grow up to **2 FT** (60 cm) **EVERY DAY.**

Americans Bruce Cantrell and Jessica Fain hold the **RECORD** for the **LONGEST NONSTOP STAY** in a fixed, underwater habitat—**73 DAYS, 2 HOURS, 34 MINUTES.**

In **1520,** explorer **FERDINAND MAGELLAN** became the **FIRST** to lead European ships into an ocean he named **PACIFIC,** meaning **"PEACEFUL."**

Canada's **BAY OF FUNDY** experiences the world's **BIGGEST DIFFERENCE BETWEEN DEPTH** at low and high tide, in some places up to **65 FT** (20 m).

In **1912,** the RMS *TITANIC* cruise liner hit an **ATLANTIC ICEBERG** and sank. Its wreckage now rests at a depth of **12,500 FT** (3,800 m).

36,070 FT (10,994 m) is the **DEEPEST-KNOWN POINT** of the oceans—located at **Challenger Deep** in the Pacific Ocean.

Australia's **Great Barrier Reef** has approximately **3,000 REEFS, 600 CORAL SPECIES,** and **3,000 TYPES OF MOLLUSK.**

REEF FISH AND MOLLUSKS provide food for **30–40 million** people every year.

DESERTS

Deserts are the driest places on Earth. They receive under 10 in (250 mm) of rainfall per year. Some are hot, while others are cold. Though deserts are harsh environments, they are home to some hardy wildlife.

Only about **20%** of Earth's **DESERTS** are covered by **SAND.**

57 MPH (92 km/h) was Henrik May's top speed **SKIING** down **NAMIB DESERT DUNES.**

DINOSAUR EGG FOSSILS discovered in the **GOBI DESERT** were about **80 MILLION YEARS OLD.**

Kangaroo rats in the Sonoran Desert in North America can leap **9 FT** (2.75 m) to **ESCAPE PREDATORS.**

In 1903, **ARICA,** a region in Chile's **Atacama Desert,** began a spell of **172 months WITHOUT** any **RAIN.**

In 2011, Iran's Reza Pakravan **CYCLED 1,077 MILES** (1,734 km) **ACROSS THE SAHARA.** It took him a record **13 DAYS, 5 HOURS, 50 MINUTES,** and **14 SECONDS.**

The world's tallest
SAGUARO CACTUS
measured **78 FT** (23.8 m) and was found in the Sonoran Desert.

The giant **RICHAT STRUCTURE**–a **DOME OF ROCK** in the Sahara Desert– has a base diameter of **28 MILES** (45 m) and **RINGS** that look like a **BULL'S-EYE** when viewed from space.

A group of **DUNES** in China **MOVED** more than **328 FT** (100 m) per year between **1954** and **1959**.

The world's **tallest sand dunes** are over **3,280 FT** (1,000 m) high.

The **LARGEST DESERT** in South America is the **PATAGONIAN DESERT** with an area of approximately **260,000 SQ MILES** (673,000 sq km).

WELWITSCHIA PLANTS
that grow in the **NAMIB DESERT** in southern Africa have an estimated **LIFESPAN** of up to **1,500 YEARS.**

The **BIGGEST TEMPERATURE** swings occur in the Gobi Desert. **AVERAGE HIGHS** reach **113°F** (45°C) while **AVERAGE LOWS** can reach **–40°F** (–40°C).

3.5 million SQ MILES
(9.2 million sq km) is the **AREA** covered by the **SAHARA** in North Africa–the world's **LARGEST HOT DESERT.**

Camels were **DOMESTICATED** in the **ARABIAN DESERT** around **5,000 YEARS AGO.** They were brought to the **SAHARA** in the **1st century.**

The **FIRST CAMEL** was imported to Australia in **1840.** Today, **MORE THAN 1,000,000 FERAL CAMELS ROAM** the deserts of **AUSTRALIA.**

330,000 TONS
of **SAND** were picked up by **GOBI DESERT SANDSTORMS** in 2006. Most of the sand settled over **BEIJING, CHINA,** more than **1,000 MILES** (1,600 km) away.

At the POLES

Earth's polar regions experience long, dark winters and freezing temperatures. The North Pole lies on drifting ice in the Arctic Ocean, while the South Pole sits within the icy Antarctic continent.

Only 1 sunset and sunrise
occur at the **NORTH POLE** each year.

32°F (0°C) at the **NORTH POLE** and **−18.76°F** (−28.2°C) at the **SOUTH POLE** are the **AVERAGE TEMPERATURES** during the **SUMMER MONTHS.**

20 million
PENGUINS live around **ANTARCTICA'S COASTS** and the **SOUTHERN OCEAN.**

98%
of land in Antarctica is **buried under snow and ice.**

There are approximately
400 lakes
hidden under Antarctica's ice sheet. The largest, **LAKE VOSTOK,** has an area of around
3,860 SQ MILES
(10,000 sq km).

12,447 FT
(3,447 m) is the height of **Antarctica's only active volcano** —Mount Erebus.

In **1986,** American explorer **ANN BANCROFT** became **the first woman** to reach the **NORTH POLE,** traveling more than
1,000 MILES
(1,600 km) by **DOGSLED.**

Antarctica's **ONLY NATIVE INSECT**— **the Antarctic midge**—spends **9 months** of the year frozen solid.

In **1911,** Norwegian explorer **ROALD AMUNDSEN** led the **FIRST EXPEDITION** to the **SOUTH POLE** with **52 DOGS.** **ONLY 12** made the return journey.

The **SPIRAL TUSK OF A NARWHAL**—a small whale that lives in the Arctic Ocean - can grow up to **10 FT** (3 m).

In **2007,** **RUSSIA'S MIR SUBMARINE** planted a flag in the **SEABED** of the Arctic Ocean, **13,979 FT** (4,261 m) directly below the **NORTH POLE.**

1,258 is the number of summer residents at **MCMURDO STATION**— the largest of **70 permanent research bases** in Antarctica.

In **1978,** Emilio Marcos Palma of Argentina became the **FIRST PERSON** to be born in Antarctica.

In **1959,** **12 NATIONS** signed the **ANTARCTIC TREATY** promising to preserve the continent for **PEACEFUL SCIENTIFIC RESEARCH** and not exploit its resources.

64.9°F (18.3°C) is the **HIGHEST TEMPERATURE** ever recorded in Antarctica, in February 2020.

The approximate **NUMBER OF PEOPLE** who live **in the Arctic** is **4 MILLION.**

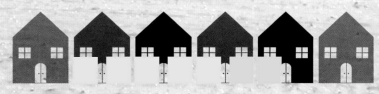

Climate and WEATHER

Weather is what's happening in the air at any given time, whether it's sunny or cloudy, rainy or dry. It is determined by wind patterns, temperature, moisture, and air pressure. Climate is the average weather a region experiences over a period of time.

A **TROPICAL CYCLONE** is classified as a hurricane if its winds reach speeds of **74 MPH** (119 km/h).

The **LARGEST TROPICAL CYCLONE** ever recorded was **TYPHOON TIP** in **1979**, with a diameter of about **1,380 MILES** (2,220 km).

Raindrops

in a light shower fall at an **AVERAGE SPEED** of **14 MPH** (22.5 km/h). The largest raindrops fall at **20 MPH** (32 km/h).

A record **12 IN** (305 mm) of rain fell in **60 MINUTES** in Missouri in **1947**.

In **2019**, there were **1,520** confirmed **TORNADOES** in the US. 77 of them occurred on **MAY 27.**

In **1972**, a **7-DAY-LONG** blizzard in Iran dumped **10–26 FT** (3–8 m) **OF SNOW** over much of the country.

Around **467 IN** (11,871 mm) of **RAIN** falls on **MAWSYNRAM, INDIA**, every year—that's the height of **2 GIRAFFES.**

US park ranger Roy Sullivan was struck **7 times** by **LIGHTNING** between 1942 and 1977.

200 MPH (320 km/h).

POINT REYES (California) and **ARGENTIA** (Newfoundland, Canada) are the **FOGGIEST** land areas in the world, with more than **200 DAYS OF FOG A YEAR.**

The strongest-intensity tornadoes feature **WIND SPEEDS** of more than

Every day,
LIGHTNING
flashes more than
3,000,000
times around the world. That's
an average of **44 LIGHTNING
STRIKES** every second.

An average **LIGHTNING BOLT** is
2–3 MILES (3–5 km)
long, but only **¾–1 IN**
(2–3 cm) wide—barely
wider than your thumb.

**19 of
the 20**
years with the
**WARMEST
GLOBAL SURFACE
TEMPERATURE**
have occurred
since 2001.
2016 and
2020 have
tied for the
**WARMEST
YEARS**
on record.

A lightning strike can heat air to
about **54,000°F** (30,000°C), causing
it to expand rapidly and create the
SOUND OF THUNDER.

The **HEAVIEST-
RECORDED HAILSTONE**
weighed **2.25 LB**
(1.02 kg) in Bangladesh
in **1986.**

In **1654,** the Italian
Medici family set up the
**FIRST WEATHER-RECORDING
NETWORK,** with **11** weather
stations dotted around Europe.

The official estimated **COST OF THE
DAMAGE** caused by **HURRICANE
KATRINA** in the US in 2005 was
$170 BILLION.

The average global
temperature in **2019**
was **2°F** (1.1°C)
higher than
250
YEARS AGO.

The **AVERAGE ANNUAL
RAINFALL** recorded in
Quillagua in the Atacama
Desert, Chile, between
1964 and 2001 was just
0.02 IN (0.5 cm).

NATURE

PREHISTORIC CREATURES

Life began on Earth more than 3.5 billion years ago and, over time, evolved to form an extraordinary variety of plants and animals. Fossils (the naturally preserved remains of animals or plants) give us a unique insight into some of the creatures that existed millions of years ago, including the mighty dinosaurs.

TYRANNOSAURUS REX could weigh up to **15,500 LB** (7,000 kg) and grow about **39 FT** (12 m) long.

ARGENTINOSAURUS, one of the largest land animals ever, was **115 FT** (35 m) long and could weigh as much as **154,000 LB** (70,000 kg)– **10 TIMES** more than a *Tyrannosaurus rex*.

QUETZALCOATLUS, the biggest pterosaur, stood as tall as a giraffe and had a **36-FT** (11-m) **WINGSPAN.**

Most of the **WOOLLY MAMMOTHS** died about **10,000 YEARS AGO,** but the last isolated mammoths died only **4,000 YEARS AGO.**

A *Tyrannosaurus rex* had **60 cone-shaped, serrated teeth,** each about **8 IN** (20 cm) long.

 **Elasmosaurus,** a plesiosaur, had **72 bones** in its **neck.**

The **skull** of a *Tyrannosaurus rex* was about **5 FT** (1.5 m) long.

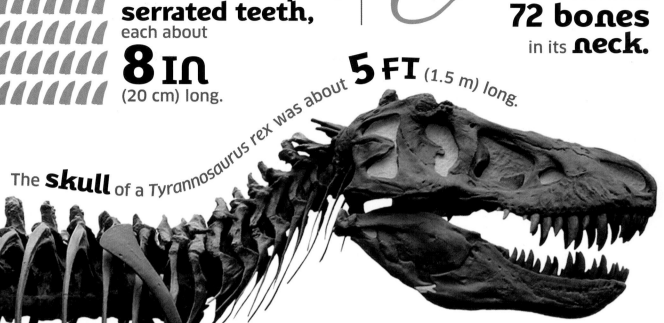

The term **dinosaur,** meaning **"FEARFULLY GREAT LIZARD,"** was coined by Sir Richard Owen in **1842.**

In **2020,** more than **200 mammoth skeletons** were found in Mexico at an airport construction site.

A T-REX SKELETON named Stan was sold for **$31.8 million** in an auction in **2020.**

The largest-known ichthyosaur, **SHONISAURUS,** could grow up to **85 FT** (26 m) long, only slightly smaller than a blue whale.

Around **700 SPECIES OF DINOSAUR** have been discovered and named.

Smilodon, a prehistoric **SABER-TOOTHED CAT,** had a pair of **11-IN-** (28-cm-) **LONG CANINE TEETH.**

In **1947,** more than **500 *Coelophysis* DINOSAUR FOSSILS** were discovered at Ghost Ranch in New Mexico.

Found in Australia, the length of the **LARGEST FOSSILIZED DINOSAUR FOOTPRINT** is **5 FT 9 IN** (1.75 m).

Microscopic LIFE

Our world is full of tiny organisms, such as bacteria, viruses, algae, fungi, lice, and mites. Though small, they can have a big and widespread impact on our lives—from helping us digest our food to spreading life-threatening diseases.

Thiovulum majus is one of the **FASTEST-MOVING BACTERIUM,** able to swim up to **60 BODY LENGTHS** a second.

CYANOBACTERIA, which evolved around **2.4 BILLION YEARS AGO,** were the first living things to **PHOTOSYNTHESIZE** (make food and oxygen from sunlight).

At least **700** different species of **BACTERIA** and other microbes **live in your mouth.**

TARDIGRADES (eight-legged microscopic animals) **CAN SURVIVE** without food and water for more than **30 YEARS.**

Caulobacter crescentus bacteria produce a **SUGAR-BASED STICKY GLUE** that forms a bond **3 times STRONGER** than superglue.

As much as **80%** of the **WORLD'S OXYGEN** is produced by **phytoplankton.**

Head lice measure 1/16–1/8 IN (2–4 mm) long and can bite you 5–6 times a day.

A single **TEASPOON OF SOIL** can contain between **100 million and 1 billion bacteria.**

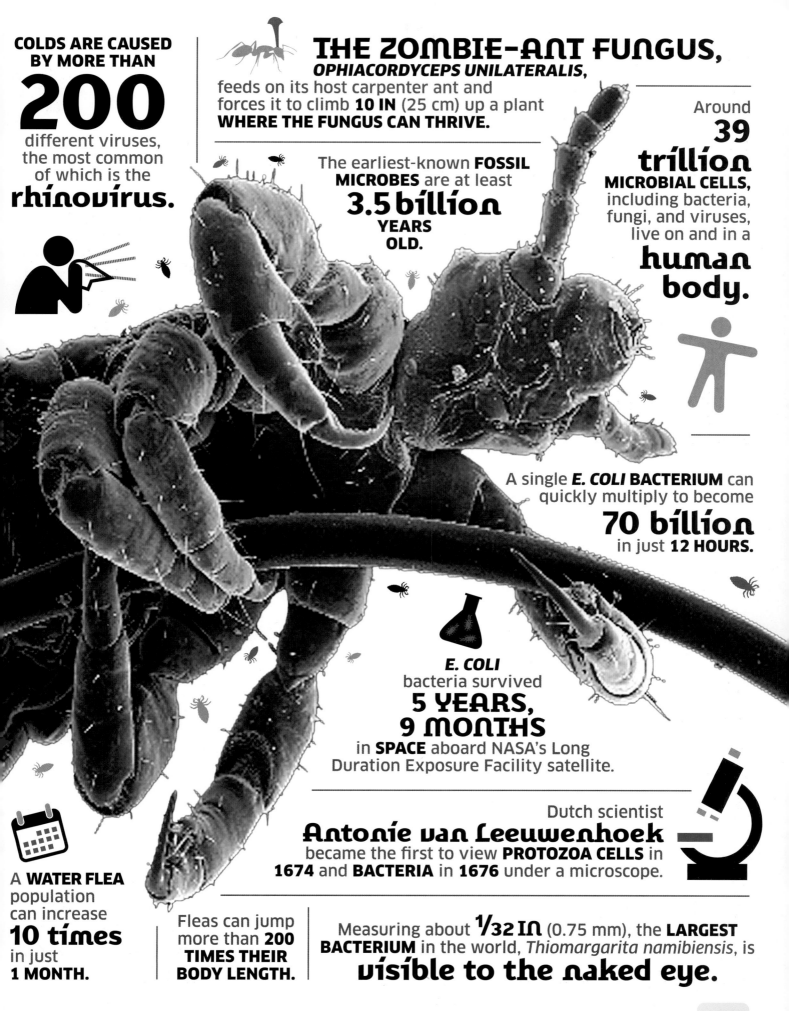

COLDS ARE CAUSED BY MORE THAN
200
different viruses, the most common of which is the
rhinovirus.

THE ZOMBIE-ANT FUNGUS,
OPHIACORDYCEPS UNILATERALIS,
feeds on its host carpenter ant and forces it to climb **10 IN** (25 cm) up a plant **WHERE THE FUNGUS CAN THRIVE.**

The earliest-known **FOSSIL MICROBES** are at least
3.5 billion
YEARS OLD.

Around
39 trillion
MICROBIAL CELLS,
including bacteria, fungi, and viruses, live on and in a
human body.

A single **E. COLI BACTERIUM** can quickly multiply to become
70 billion
in just **12 HOURS.**

E. COLI
bacteria survived
5 YEARS, 9 MONTHS
in **SPACE** aboard NASA's Long Duration Exposure Facility satellite.

Dutch scientist
Antonie van Leeuwenhoek
became the first to view **PROTOZOA CELLS** in **1674** and **BACTERIA** in **1676** under a microscope.

A **WATER FLEA** population can increase
10 times
in just **1 MONTH.**

Fleas can jump more than **200 TIMES THEIR BODY LENGTH.**

Measuring about **1/32 IN** (0.75 mm), the **LARGEST BACTERIUM** in the world, *Thiomargarita namibiensis*, is
visible to the naked eye.

Fabulous FLORA

There are at least 350,000 species of plants, from nonflowering ferns and towering trees to fragrant roses and delicate daisies. Plants produce some of the oxygen we need to breathe through a process called photosynthesis, and many animals rely on plants as their main source of food.

Some species of bamboo grow up to **35 IN** (91 cm) in a day, making them the **FASTEST-GROWING PLANTS** in the world.

A single **RAGWEED PLANT** can produce up to **1 BILLION** grains of pollen.

Just **15 PLANTS,** including rice, maize, and wheat, provide **90% of the food energy** intake of the world's population.

There are about **200 seeds** found in a **STRAWBERRY,** unusually all on the **OUTSIDE.**

The desert plant **WELWITSCHIA** has **only 2 leaves,** which can grow up to **13 FT** (4 m) long. These help the plant **TAKE MOISTURE** from fog.

The circular leaves of the **AMAZON WATER LILY** can measure up to **8 FT** (2.5 m) and support up to **100 LB** (45 kg) of weight on water.

The **TITAN ARUM** has the **TALLEST FLOWER SPIKE** in the world, measuring **10 FT** (3 m) in height.

THE EARLIEST-KNOWN FLOWERING PLANT—the aquatic *Montsechia vidalii*—lived around **130 million years ago.**

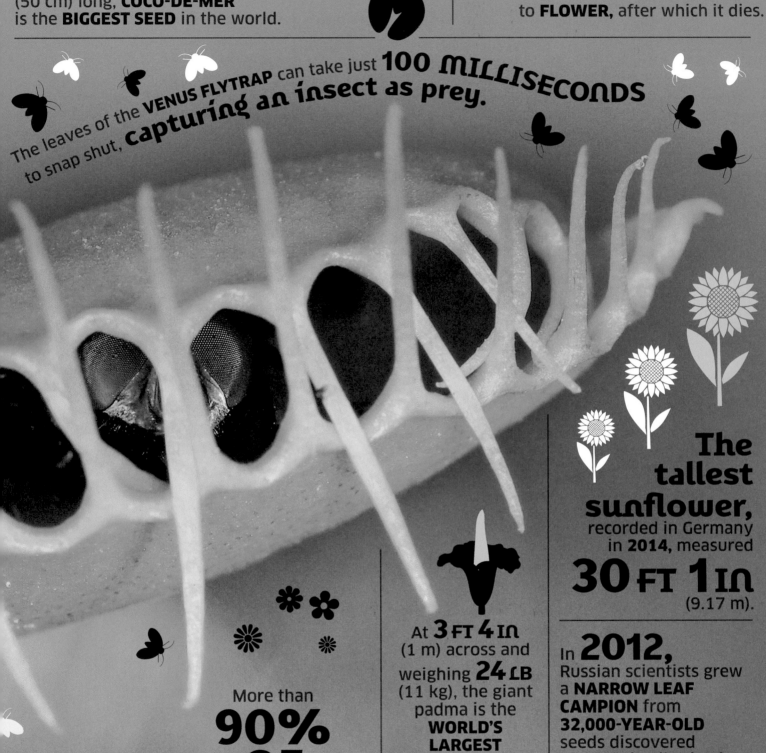

Weighing up to **55 LB** (25 kg) and growing up to **1 FT 7 IN** (50 cm) long, **COCO-DE-MER** is the **BIGGEST SEED** in the world.

One species of **AGAVE** can take more than **25 YEARS** to **FLOWER**, after which it dies.

The leaves of the **VENUS FLYTRAP** can take just **100 MILLISECONDS** to snap shut, **capturing an insect as prey.**

The tallest sunflower, recorded in Germany in **2014**, measured **30 FT 1 IN** (9.17 m).

At **3 FT 4 IN** (1 m) across and weighing **24 LB** (11 kg), the giant padma is the **WORLD'S LARGEST SINGLE FLOWER.**

In **2012**, Russian scientists grew a **NARROW LEAF CAMPION** from **32,000-YEAR-OLD** seeds discovered **FROZEN** in Siberian ice.

1,942 NEW SPECIES of plants were scientifically named **in 2019.**

More than **90% OF ALL PLANTS** are **FLOWERING PLANTS.**

To aid **DISPERSAL BY WIND**, each seed of a **JAVAN CUCUMBER** is encased in a transparent **4¾-IN-** (12-cm-) wide **WING.**

Spiders, bugs, and
INSECTS

Our planet is packed with insects and other creepy-crawlies, such as spiders, millipedes, bugs, and ticks. They make up more than 90 percent of all the animal species in the world. Millions of years ago, insects were the first animals to fly. Today, they are found in almost all habitats of the world.

DARWIN BARK SPIDERS
can spin **WEBS** across rivers up to **82 FT** (25 m) wide.

LEAF-CUTTING ANTS
can **LIFT** up to **50 TIMES** their own **BODY WEIGHT**.

HOUSE FLIES
taste using their **FEET**, which are **10,000 TIMES MORE SENSITIVE** than the human tongue.

Each **COMPOUND EYE** of a **DRAGONFLY** can contain up to **30,000** lenses.

1 MILLIONTH OF A GRAM of venom from a **BRAZILIAN WANDERING SPIDER** can kill **41 MICE.**

HONEYBEES beat their wings **250 TIMES IN A SECOND.**

GIANT STICK INSECTS
are some of the **LONGEST INSECTS** in the world, growing up to **20 IN** (50 cm) in length.

THE WOOLLY BEAR CATERPILLAR
found in the Arctic **FREEZES SOLID** in winter and can take up to **14 YEARS** to transform into a **MOTH.**

At **0.006 IN** (0.15 mm) in length, the *KIKIKI HUNA*, a species of fairyfly wasp, is the world's **SMALLEST FLYING INSECT.**

BEES fly about
55,000 MILES
(88,500 km)–more than twice the distance around Earth–to make **JUST 1 JAR OF HONEY.**

The world's leggiest living thing is the
MILLIPEDE
ILLACME PLENIPES–females can have up to **750 LEGS**, whereas the males have up to **562.**

The **CATERPILLAR** of the **POLYPHEMUS MOTH** can eat
86,000 times
its own weight in just under **2 MONTHS.**

The **LENGTH** of one of the **SMALLEST SPIDERS** in the world, **PATU DIGUA**, is
0.014 IN
(0.37 mm) – roughly equal to the size of a **PINHEAD.**

The **DRACULA ANT** shuts its **MANDIBLES** (jaws) at speeds of up to
295 FT
(90 m) per second.

The **WINGSPAN** of the **WORLD'S LARGEST BUTTERFLY**–Queen Alexandra's birdwing– is **12 IN** (30 cm).

A HORNED DUNG BEETLE can pull **1,141** times its own body weight.

Froghoppers
can **JUMP** up to **28 IN** (70 cm) into the air, accelerating with a force **400 TIMES** that of gravity.

Some species of **PERIODICAL CICADAS** live underground for
13 or 17 YEARS
before **EMERGING** as adults.

The leg span of a
GOLIATH BIRD-EATING TARANTULA IS 11 IN
(28 cm)–about the size of a **DINNER PLATE.**

Fantastic FISH

More than 33,000 species of fish live in saltwater seas and freshwater lakes and rivers around the world. They range in size from as small as a fingernail to as large as a bus. Fish breathe underwater using gills, and many have slippery scales to help them move easily through the water.

A **NORTHERN SNAKEHEAD** fish can breathe air and live **OUT OF WATER** for up to **4 days.**

MALE SEAHORSES carry the female's eggs and give birth to **50—1,500 babies,** known as fry.

A **RED LIONFISH'S STOMACH** can **EXPAND** up to **30 TIMES** its normal size after eating.

It takes a **FROGFISH** just **0.006 seconds to consume its prey.**

COELACANTHS were thought to have been **EXTINCT FOR 65 MILLION YEARS,** until one was caught off the coast of South Africa in **1938.**

A **STRIPED MARLIN** can grow up to **13 FT 9 IN** (4.2 m) long.

An archerfish shoots a **WATER JET** with a range of **6 FT 6 IN** (2 m) **OUT OF ITS MOUTH** to knock insects into the water.

Found at depths of **26,247 FT** (8,000 m), the **MARIANA SNAILFISH** is the **WORLD'S DEEPEST-DWELLING FISH.**

The **MAXIMUM SPEED** of the sailfish— the **FASTEST FISH IN THE OCEAN**—is **68 MPH** (110 km/h).

An **ELECTRIC EEL** can fire a shock of **500 VOLTS** to stun its prey.

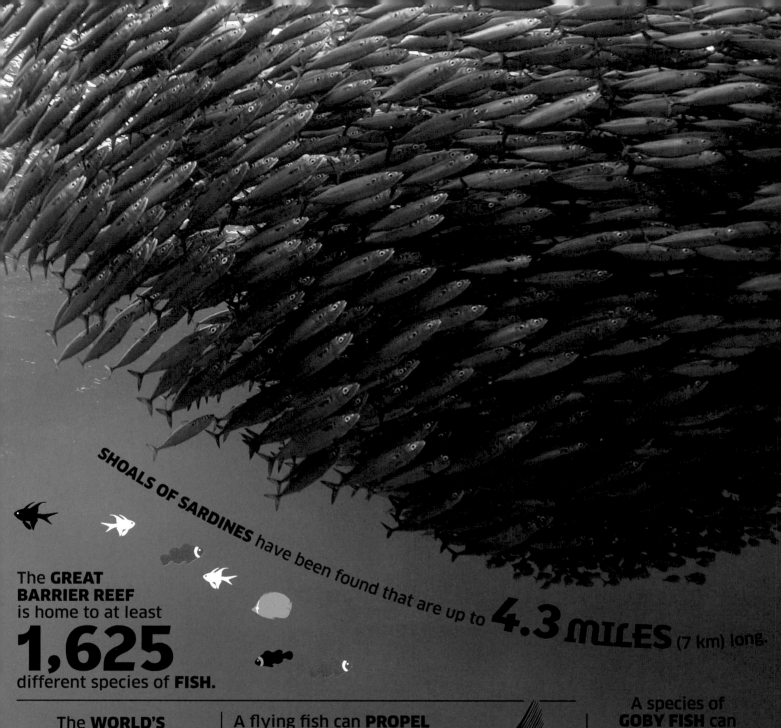

SHOALS OF SARDINES have been found that are up to **4.3 MILES** (7 km) long.

The **GREAT BARRIER REEF** is home to at least

1,625

different species of **FISH**.

The **WORLD'S SMALLEST FISH,** *Paedocypris progenetica,* measures

5/16 IN

(7.9 mm) long.

A flying fish can **PROPEL ITSELF OUT OF THE WATER** at speeds of up to

44 MPH

(72 km/h) and then **GLIDE THROUGH THE AIR** for up to **1,312 FT** (400 m).

A species of **GOBY FISH** can climb waterfalls of

330 FT

(100 m) using its **MOUTH AND BELLY SUCKERS.**

It takes a **PUFFER FISH**
10 seconds
to inflate.

An ocean sunfish can lay

300 MILLION

EGGS IN ONE GO.

ORANGE ROUGHY fish can live for more than

140 YEARS.

Rays and SHARKS

Unlike most other fish, sharks and rays have skeletons made of cartilage. Sharks often have sharp teeth, while rays are flat-bodied with long, venomous tails. There are more than 500 species of sharks and 600 species of rays.

A **SANDBAR SHARK** can grow and shed **35,000 teeth** over the course of its lifetime.

Despite their reputation, **SHARK ATTACKS** on humans are rare. Only **57 attacks** and **10 DEATHS** were documented in **2020.**

A whale shark—THE WORLD'S LARGEST FISH—can grow up to 62 FT (19 m) in length.

SHARKS HAVE EXISTED for at least **400 MILLION YEARS,** long before **DINOSAURS** evolved.

The **FASTEST SHARK** is the **SHORTFIN MAKO,** which can swim at speeds of over **35 MPH** (56 km/h).

A **GREAT WHITE SHARK'S MOUTH** contains **300** triangular **SERRATED TEETH,** each up to **3 IN** (7.5 cm) long.

The **SMALLEST MALE SHARKS** are those of the **DWARF LANTERN SHARK,** which measure **JUST 6 IN** (16 cm) long.

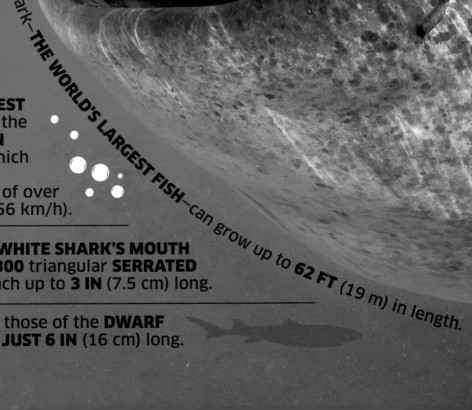

MOBULA RAYS can leap

6 FT 6 IN (2 m)

above the water's surface, landing with a resounding **BELLY FLOP.**

Many of the

200

different species of **STINGRAY** can **CRUSH** clams and other mollusk shells with their **JAWS.**

In **2016,** scientists announced that a **LIVING GREENLAND SHARK** was approximately

400 YEARS OLD.

The great white shark

can smell odors as small as

1 part per 25 million.

It can detect a faint scent

MORE THAN 1,640 FT

(500 m) away.

The release of **STEVEN SPIELBERG'S BLOCKBUSTER** *JAWS* in **1975** escalated people's fear of all sharks as predatory killers. Only

6% of species

have ever **ATTACKED HUMANS.**

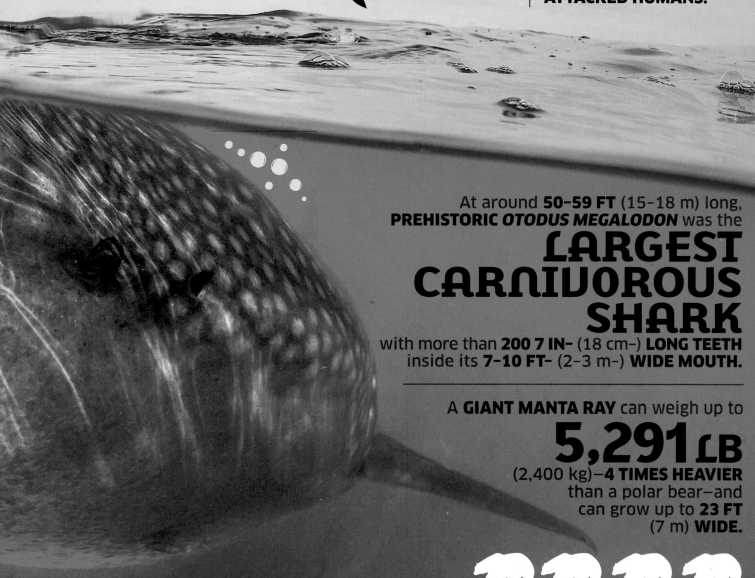

At around **50–59 FT** (15–18 m) long, **PREHISTORIC** *OTODUS MEGALODON* was the

LARGEST CARNIVOROUS SHARK

with more than **200 7 IN–** (18 cm–) **LONG TEETH** inside its **7–10 FT–** (2–3 m–) **WIDE MOUTH.**

A **GIANT MANTA RAY** can weigh up to

5,291 LB

(2,400 kg)–**4 TIMES HEAVIER** than a polar bear–and can grow up to **23 FT** (7 m) **WIDE.**

Scaly REPTILES

From the smallest geckos to the mightiest crocodiles, more than 10,000 species of reptiles live on land and in the sea. These cold-blooded creatures mostly lay eggs, although some give birth to live young.

A **GAVIAL'S** long, **NARROW SNOUT** is filled with more than **100** needle-sharp, interlocking **TEETH.**

The world's **oldest land animal,** **A SEYCHELLES GIANT TORTOISE** named Jonathan, celebrated its **190th birthday** in **2022.**

A **BLACK MAMBA'S VENOM** can kill a human in just **20 MINUTES.**

Many lizardlike **TUATARAS** live to be more than **100.**

The **6.5 MILLION** microscopic hairs, called **SETAE,** on the feet of geckos allow them to **SCALE WALLS** and **HANG** from ceilings.

The Rosette-nosed **PYGMY CHAMELEON'S** tongue shoots out **2.5 times** the length of its body.

An **alligator snapping turtle** can **BITE** with a force of **1,000 LB** (450 kg), which can snap through a **HUMAN BONE.**

The **LARGEST GREEN ANACONDA**—the world's heaviest snake—to ever be recorded weighed

500 LB

(227 kg) and measured

27 FT 7 IN

(8.43 m) long.

A **GREEN SEA TURTLE** can **HOLD ITS BREATH** for
MORE THAN 5 HOURS
under water, during which its **HEARTBEAT** may **SLOW DOWN** to as little as
1 beat every 9 minutes.

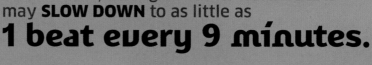

Measuring a mere
5/8 IN
(1.6 cm) long, the **SMALLEST LIZARD** in the world is so tiny that it can fit on **A COIN.**

The **GREEN BASILISK LIZARD** can **RUN ACROSS WATER** at speeds of
7 MPH
(11.3 km/h) for distances up to 16 ft (5 m). It's also a **GOOD SWIMMER** and can stay submerged for **10 MINUTES.**

For **41 years,** Lonesome George, the **PINTA ISLAND TORTOISE,** was the **LAST REMAINING MEMBER** of its species.

The **GABOON VIPER'S** fangs are
2 IN
(5 cm) long—the **LONGEST** of any snake.

TREE-DWELLING PIT VIPERS found in Southeast Asia can grow up to 3 FT (95 cm) long.

An inland taipan snake's **BITE** contains **ENOUGH VENOM** to kill more than
250,000 mice.

The saltwater crocodile is the **HEAVIEST REPTILE** in the world, weighing as much as
2,200 LB
(1,000 kg).

TOP 10
LONGEST SNAKES

1 **RETICULATED PYTHON** • *Malayopython reticulatus* • **33 FT** (10 m) • Southeast Asia

Found in forests and wetlands, these giant snakes can weigh more than 308 lb (140 kg). They ambush and then squeeze their prey, which includes birds, deer, and other mammals.

2 **GREEN ANACONDA** • *Eunectes murinus*
26–30 FT (8–9 m) • Northern South America

Unlike most snakes, green anacondas give birth to live young instead of laying eggs.

3 **AMETHYSTINE PYTHON** • *Morelia amethistina*
28 FT (8.5 m) • Indonesia, Australia, Papua New Guinea, Phillipines

A slender snake, the Amethystine python has iridescent scales that shimmer purple in the sunlight.

4 **AFRICAN ROCK PYTHON** • *Python sebae*
23 FT (7 m) • Sub-Saharan Africa

Known for its ferocity, the African rock python's prey includes mammals as big as antelopes and warthogs.

5 **BURMESE PYTHON** • *Python bivittatus*
18 FT 10 IN (5.74 m) • India, Southeast Asia, China

The Burmese python can stretch its jaws wide enough to gulp down animals five times as wide as its head.

6 **KING COBRA** • *Ophiophagus hannah*
18 FT 9 IN (5.71 m) • India, Southeast Asia, China

The venom in a king cobra's bite could kill 20 people, making it the world's longest venomous snake.

7 **INDIAN ROCK PYTHON** • *Python molurus*
13–16 FT 5 IN (4–5 m) • South Asia

Female Indian rock pythons incubate their clutches of up to 100 eggs by shivering to produce heat.

8 **YELLOW ANACONDA** • *Eunectes notaeus*
15 FT (4.6 m) • Southern South America

Female yellow anacondas can grow up to twice the length of males of the species.

9 **BOA CONSTRICTOR** • *Boa constrictor*
14 FT (4.3 m) • South America, Central America

Like many other snakes, the boa constrictor hunts by wrapping its body around prey until the creature suffocates.

10 **BLACK MAMBA** • *Dendroaspis polylepis*
14 FT (4.3 m) • Sub-Saharan Africa

When threatened, the black mamba hisses and opens its dark black mouth—the source of its name.

Amazing AMPHIBIANS

At home on land and in water, amphibians get their name from the Greek word for "both lives." There are more than 8,300 amphibian species, including frogs, toads, newts, salamanders, and caecilians.

Cave-dwelling salamanders
called **OLMS** can go **WITHOUT FOOD** for up to **10 YEARS.**

THE LARGEST CAECILIAN, *Caecilia thompsoni*, can grow **UP TO 60 IN** (152 cm) long.

A GOLDEN POISON DART FROG
contains enough **TOXIN TO KILL 10 PEOPLE** or **20,000 MICE.**

In 1935, **102 CANE TOADS** were imported into Australia to tackle cane beetle pests. By **2010**, their **POPULATION** had grown to **more than 200 million.**

In India, the **PURPLE FROG** spends **50 WEEKS** every year deep underground, surfacing only for **2 WEEKS** at the start of monsoon season to **BREED.**

The world's largest amphibian
the **CHINESE GIANT SALAMANDER**, measures around **6 FT** (1.8 m) long and weighs around **132 LB** (60 kg).

The **AFRICAN GOLIATH**
is the
WORLD'S LARGEST FROG.
It can weigh up to
7.2 LB
(3.3 kg) and
measure around
12 IN
(30 cm).

THE **AUSTRALIAN STRIPED ROCKET FROG** can leap
50 times
its **BODY LENGTH**.

A female **GREAT CRESTED NEWT** can lay up to
600 EGGS
in a breeding season.

The **AXOLOTL**, a salamander from Mexico, can **REGROW AN ENTIRE LIMB** in
2 MONTHS.

THE AFRICAN BULLFROG hibernates underground for
10 months
every year during the dry season.

RED-EYED TREE FROGS use their **6-sided** toe suckers to stay in place while sleeping.

The **MOUTH** of an **ARGENTINE HORNED FROG**, also known as the **PACMAN FROG**, makes up
half of its 6-IN-
(15-cm-) **LONG BODY**.

THE WORLD'S SMALLEST FROG, *Paedophryne amanuensis*, measures just
5/16 IN (7.7 mm).

The tree-dwelling **WALLACE'S FLYING FROG** can **GLIDE** up to **49 FT** (15 m) using its webbed feet.

At **10 IN** (25 cm), the **TADPOLE** of a **PARADOXICAL FROG** is
4 TIMES
larger than the **ADULT FROG**.

The male **DARWIN'S FROG** broods tadpoles in its vocal sac for
50—70 DAYS.

The world of
BIRDS

With around 10,000 species, birds come in all shapes and sizes—from tiny hummingbirds to towering ostriches. They are the only living animals with feathers, and most are capable of flight. All birds lay eggs with hard shells and have wings, even those that can't fly.

The fastest bird in level flight, the **WHITE-THROATED NEEDLETAIL SWIFT,** can travel at speeds of **105 MPH** (170 km/h).

SOCIABLE WEAVER BIRDS build the **LARGEST NEST** —big enough to house as many as

400 BIRDS.

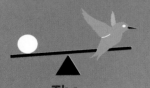

The **bee hummingbird** weighs
0.06 oz
(1.6 g)—less than a table tennis ball.

The **WINGSPAN** of an
ANDEAN CONDOR
—the largest bird of prey—is
10 FT
(3 m).

Weighing as little as
0.6 OZ (17 g), the
NORTHERN WHEATEAR SONGBIRD flies up to
9,300 MILES
(15,000 km) between Alaska and Africa each year.

In steep dives,
peregrine falcons
can reach speeds of more than
199 MPH
(320 km/h), making them the world's fastest animal.

The length of a peacock's
train of feathers
is **6 FT** (1.8 m), making up more than
60%
of its **BODY LENGTH.**

Clark's nutcracker
birds can bury more than
30,000 seeds
in autumn.

Ostriches
can grow up to
9 FT
(2.75 m) **TALL,** with their neck making up almost **HALF OF THEIR HEIGHT.**

To keep warm in their cold habitat, the **TUNDRA SWAN** has more than **25,000 feathers.**

An adult **SNOWY OWL** can eat more than **1,600 lemmings in a year.**

The **MALE WHITE BELLBIRD'S CALL** can reach a deafening **125 decibels** —louder than some rock concerts.

HUMMINGBIRDS beat their wings up to **200 times** a second.

With a **WINGSPAN** of **11 FT 6 IN** (3.5 m), the **WANDERING ALBATROSS** can fly more than **600 MILES** (1,000 km) in a single day.

There are **700 notes per minute** in the complex **SONG OF A EUROPEAN WREN.**

The **GREAT SNIPE** is the **fastest migrating bird,** with a top speed of **60 MPH** (97 km/h). It travels around **4,225 MILES** (6,800 miles) **each year.**

A **TOUCAN'S BEAK** measures **7½ IN** (19 cm)—the **BIGGEST BEAK** of any bird relative to body length.

RÜPPELL'S VULTURE can fly at an altitude of **37,000 FT** (11,280 m)— **2,000 FT** (600 m) **HIGHER THAN A PASSENGER PLANE.**

An **EMPEROR PENGUIN** can dive more than **1,640 FT** (500 m) to reach the seabed for food.

Incredible
BIG CATS

These stealthy predators are among the most beautiful, deadly, and threatened animals on the planet. They use agility, speed, and explosive power to hunt prey. There are seven species of big cats: lions, tigers, jaguars, leopards, snow leopards, cheetahs, and cougars.

A **CHEETAH** can accelerate from

0 to 60 MPH
(0 to 96 km/h) in **3 SECONDS**.

THE DARKER A LION'S MANE, the older he is. Wild lions typically live

13—15 YEARS.

SNOW LEOPARDS
live at **ALTITUDES** as high as

19,222 FT
(5,859 m) above sea level—**HIGHER THAN ANY OTHER** big cat.

A **TIGER'S NIGHT VISION** is

6 times
better than a human's.

There are

9
SUBSPECIES OF TIGER, 3 of which (Bali, Caspian, and Javan) are already **EXTINCT.**

A LION'S ROAR
can be heard

3—5 MILES
(5-8 km) away.

Like all big cats, **JAGUAR CUBS** are **BORN BLIND** and gain **SIGHT** only after

14 DAYS.

WILD TIGER ROAMING TERRITORY has shrunk by

96%
in the last

150 years.

A **lioness** can run at up to

50 MPH
(81 km/h).

The **JAGUAR** is the **biggest** cat in the **AMERICAS**— measuring up to **5.6 FT** (1.7 m) long and weighing

265 LB
(120 kg).

JAGUARS ROAM UP TO

6.2 MILES
(10 km) per night in search of **PREY.**

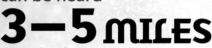

MALE SIBERIAN TIGERS are the **LARGEST BIG CATS**, growing up to **10.8 FT** (3.3 m) long and weighing **675 LB** (306 kg).

As few as
23,000 lions exist
in the wild. A century ago, that figure was
200,000.

A **MALE LION** can eat up to
88 LB
(40 kg) of **MEAT** in a single sitting— over
15%
of its body weight.

A **TIGER** typically **SLEEPS** for
15.8 HOURS PER DAY.

A **LEOPARD** can **DRAG THE BODY** of an animal
2 or 3 TIMES
its own size up a tree to keep it away from scavengers.

A **CHEETAH** can run a **100-M RACE** in
5.95 seconds
—almost **TWICE** as fast as Usain Bolt's **9.58-SECOND WORLD RECORD.**

COUGAR KITTENS are born with
BLACK SPOTS
that disappear at around
6 months.

The magnificent
WHALE

These water-dwelling mammals are some of the world's largest animals. They are found in every ocean, from the warm tropics to icy polar seas.

23 FT
(7 m) is the average width of a blue whale's **tail fluke.**

The **BOWHEAD WHALE** has the **LARGEST MOUTH** of any animal, around **8 FT** (2.4 m) wide and **16 FT** (4.9 m) long–the length of **3 ADULT HUMANS.**

Humpback whale **CALVES** can drink **160 GALLONS** (600 liters) of **MILK** a day.

A **HUMPBACK WHALE** weighs up to **40 TONS.**

There are **2 TYPES** of whale—**BALEEN** and **TOOTHED.**

SPERM WHALES can reach depths of **2 MILES** (3 km) when diving for prey.

The **BLUE WHALE** can grow to be more than **100 FT** (30 m) long.

The **HEART** of a **BLUE WHALE** can weigh **440 LB** (200 kg), the **LARGEST** in the animal kingdom.

BLUE WHALES can **FILTER** **8,000 LB** (3,630 kg) **OF KRILL** per day with **LONG BRISTLES** in their mouth called **BALEEN**.

There are around **90** known **SPECIES** of **WHALES, DOLPHINS**, and **PORPOISES**.

CUVIER'S BEAKED WHALES can **HOLD THEIR BREATH** for up to **3 hours, 42 minutes** during deep dives.

BLUE WHALE CALVES can weigh **5,960 LB** (2,700 kg) and are about **26 FT** (8 m) long.

Sperm whales can **SLEEP UPRIGHT** at depths of **33 FT** (10 m).

A **humpback whale's "song"** is made from **DIFFERENT SOUNDS** and can last for **35 minutes.**

HUMPBACK WHALES leap high **OUT OF THE WATER** at speeds of up to **17 MPH** (27 km/h).

Humpback whales **MIGRATE TO WARMER WATERS** to breed, covering a distance of about **5,150 MILES** (8,300 km) each way.

The sperm whale has the **BIGGEST BRAIN** of any animal, weighing around **17 LB** (7.8 kg).

BOWHEAD WHALES can live for **200 YEARS.**

BLUE WHALES can weigh more than **165 tons,** which is equal to the weight of **32 Asian elephants.**

Brawny
BEARS

These magnificent mammals are surprisingly agile, good climbers, and, in some cases, expert swimmers. Bears can be found on every continent except Africa, Australia, and Antarctica.

There are

8

SPECIES OF BEARS.
A 9th, the Atlas bear—the **ONLY AFRICAN SPECIES**— became extinct in

THE LATE 19TH CENTURY.

Less than 2% of hunts by a **POLAR BEAR** are **SUCCESSFUL.**

A **GRIZZLY BEAR** can catch **more than 30 salmon a day** during **SALMON SPAWNING SEASON.**

In **2011** there were reports of a **POLAR BEAR** making a **CONTINUOUS SWIM** of **427 MILES** (687 km) over a period of **232 HOURS** in the Beaufort Sea.

Grizzly bears in the western US **FEAST** on up to

40,000

ARMY CUTWORM MOTHS a day.

The **ONLY BEAR** species in **SOUTH AMERICA** is the **SPECTACLED BEAR.** It mostly eats **FRUITS, PLANTS, AND BULBS—**

only 5%

of its **DIET** is made up of **MEAT.**

GIANT PANDAS have to **EAT FOR 10—16 HOURS A DAY** to digest the nutrients they need. They consume **UP TO 38% OF THEIR BODY WEIGHT IN BAMBOO EACH DAY.**

The average **BIRTH WEIGHT** of a **GIANT PANDA** is

3.5 oz

(100 g). That's

1/900th

the weight of its mother.

A **BLACK BEAR'S HEART RATE** can **DROP** from **40–50** to just

8 BEATS PER MINUTE

during their winter **DEEP SLEEP.**

MALE GRIZZLY BEARS

can weigh up to

800 LB

(360 kg).

With a **TOP SPEED OF**

25–30 MPH

(40–50 km/h) over short distances, **HUMANS CANNOT OUTRUN A BLACK BEAR.**

A **SUN BEAR'S** tongue is **8–10 IN** (20–25 cm) long. It's used to extract **HONEY FROM BEEHIVES.**

From a distance of **MORE THAN 3,280 FT** (1,000 m), **POLAR BEARS** can **SNIFF OUT** a seal, even when it's hidden **BENEATH 3 FT 3 IN** (1 m) of

SOLID ICE.

BLACK BEARS

put on as much as

30 LB

(13.6 kg) **IN WEIGHT PER WEEK** in summer and early autumn prior to their winter sleep.

There are around **26,000** polar bears **REMAINING IN THE WILD.**

SLOTH BEARS live in Sri Lanka and India. Growing up to **6 FT 6 IN** (2 m) long, they carry their young on their backs until they are

6–9

MONTHS OLD.

PRIMATES

There are more than 400 species of primates, ranging from tiny dwarf lemurs and goggle-eyed tarsiers to resourceful chimpanzees and giant gorillas. These remarkable mammals vary greatly, but most primates have well-developed brains and dextrous hands.

There are **5 TYPES** of **GREAT APES**: gorillas, chimpanzees, orangutans, bonobos, **and us!**

A **TARSIER'S** **½-IN-** (16-mm-) wide **EYEBALL** is the **SAME SIZE** as its **BRAIN**.

SQUIRREL MONKEYS use at least **26 different calls** to **COMMUNICATE** with their local group.

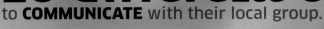

Found in Asia **300,000– 2,000,000 YEARS AGO**, the extinct ape *GIGANTOPITHECUS BLACKI* stood **10 FT** (3 m) **TALL** and may have **WEIGHED** up to **1,100 LB** (500 kg).

Orangutans have one of the **LONGEST childhoods** of any animal, with infants nursed by their mother for **6 YEARS.**

An **AYE-AYE** has **6 DIGITS** on its hands. They include a tiny **FALSE THUMB** that helps with gripping, and an **OVERLONG FINGER** used to tap on trees up to **11 TIMES** a second to detect insects underneath.

The **SLOW LORIS** has **2 TONGUES.** Its under-tongue, or **SUBLINGUAL**, is used to **clean its front TEETH.**

The **PATAS MONKEY** can run up to **34 MPH** (55 km/h), making it the **FASTEST MONKEY** in the world.

Ring-tailed lemurs have **13 BLACK-AND-WHITE BANDS** around their tails. Males wipe their tails with **FOUL-SMELLING SUBSTANCES** from scent glands and wave their tails at rivals in **STINK FIGHTS.**

The **OLDEST-KNOWN CHIMPANZEE,** Little Mama, was **76–82 years old** when she died in 2017.

Weighing **1–1.5 OZ** (25–38 g), the **PYGMY MOUSE LEMUR** is the **SMALLEST PRIMATE** in the world.

A male **MANDRILL** has **TEETH** up to **2½ IN** (6.5 cm) **long.**

A newborn **BABY GORILLA** weighs **3–4 LB** (1.4–1.8 kg), about **half** the birth weight of a **typical human.**

The **nose** of a **PROBOSCIS MONKEY** can grow up to **7 IN** (17.5 cm) long.

ORANGUTANS spend about **80–90%** of their **TIME UP TREES.**

Research scientists taught **KOKO,** a **WESTERN LOWLAND GORILLA,** to understand more than **1,000 WORDS** in **SIGN LANGUAGE.**

The Hainan gibbon is the world's **RAREST PRIMATE.** Fewer than **30** are thought to be left in the wild.

TOP 10 HEAVIEST LAND ANIMALS

1 **AFRICAN SAVANNA ELEPHANT** • *Loxodonta africana*
8,100–15,500 LB (4,000–7,000 kg)
Central and southern Africa

The heaviest animal on land, African elephants feed for 18 hours a day to fuel their giant bodies. They are an endangered species, with fewer than 315,000 left in the wild.

2 **AFRICAN FOREST ELEPHANT** • *Loxodonta cyclotis* • **6,000–13,200 LB** (2,700–6,000 kg) • West and central Africa

Extensive illegal poaching and low reproduction rates have caused the African forest elephant to become critically endangered.

3 **ASIAN ELEPHANT** • *Elephas maximus* • **6,600–11,000 LB** (3,000–5,000 kg) • South Asia, Southeast Asia

The Asian elephant has smaller ears than its African relatives and roams through cooler jungle habitats.

4 **WHITE RHINOCEROS** • *Ceratotherium simum* • **4,000–5,500 LB** (1,800–2,500 kg) • Central and southern Africa

Made up of two subspecies, the white rhinoceros is threatened by poaching. Only two northern white rhinos survive today.

5 **WALRUS** • *Odobenus rosmarus* • **2,600–4,400 LB** (1,200–2,000 kg) Arctic regions of North America, Europe, and Asia

Insulating fat called blubber makes up a large part of a walrus's weight and keeps it warm in Arctic seas.

6 **JAVAN RHINOCEROS** • *Rhinoceros sondaicus* • **2,000–5,000 LB** (900–2,300 kg) • Southeast Asia

The rare Javan rhinoceros has gray-brown skin and a sharp horn that can grow up to 10 in (25 cm) long.

7 **HIPPOPOTAMUS** • *Hippopotamus amphibius* • **3,100–3,300 LB** (1,400–1,500 kg) • Central and southern Africa

This aggressive plant-eater has the biggest mouth of any land animal and is known to attack humans.

8 **GIRAFFE** • *Giraffa camelopardalis* • **1,300–4,200 LB** (600–1,900 kg) Central and southern Africa

With a towering neck and long legs, the giraffe can grow up to 18 ft (5.5 m) tall, allowing it to reach its favorite leaves in tall acacia trees.

9 **BLACK RHINOCEROS** • *Diceros bicornis* • **2,000–3000 LB** (900–1,350 kg) • Central and southern Africa

A critically endangered species, black rhinos feed on leaves at night and sleep during the hot African days.

10 **WILD WATER BUFFALO** • *Bubalus arnee* • **1,750–2,600 LB** (800–1,200 kg) • South Asia, Southeast Asia

The wild water buffalo lives in herds and likes to bask in muddy or watery habitats to keep cool and deter flies and other pests.

More than half of all the bones in the body are found in the **HANDS AND FEET**—

27

in each **HAND** and

26

in each **FOOT**.

Laid end-to-end, all the **blood vessels** in the body would stretch roughly

60,000 MILES

(100,000 km)—about **2.5 TIMES EARTH'S CIRCUMFERENCE.**

The **masseter muscle** is the **STRONGEST MUSCLE IN THE BODY**—it can close the jaw with a **BITE FORCE** of up to

200 LB

(91 kg).

Up to **3.2 PINTS** (1.5 liters) of

GASTRIC JUICE

containing **HYDROCHLORIC ACID** is secreted inside the stomach per day.

The spine **COMPRESSES** during the day and **STRETCHES OUT** while we sleep, which means we are

⅜ IN

(1 cm) **TALLER** in the morning than when we go to bed.

A PAIR OF LUNGS contains more than

300 million

AIR SACS called alveoli.

There are **360 joints** in the human body that help us to **move and bend.**

The **VERTEBRAL** (or spinal) **COLUMN** is a stack of

33

ROUNDED BONES called vertebrae.

Our body makes about **3.2 PINTS** (1.5 liters) **OF URINE** every day—enough to fill

6 cups.

The **KIDNEYS** filter approximately **420 PINTS** (200 liters) of **BLOOD** every **24 hours.**

The **23-FT-** (7-m-) long **SMALL INTESTINE** is the longest part of the **DIGESTIVE SYSTEM.**

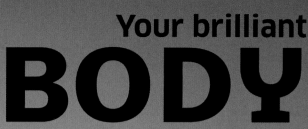

The human body is made up of trillions of cells, which group together to form organs, bones, and tissues. These work together in vast networks that carry out vital functions—from digesting food to transporting blood around the body.

The **DNA** in a single **HUMAN CELL** would measure **6 FT** (1.8 m) long if it were stretched out.

Humans are born with nearly **300 BONES,** but as we grow, some bones **FUSE TOGETHER.** Adults typically have **206 BONES.**

The **GLUTEUS MAXIMUS** in the buttocks is the largest of more than **650 MUSCLES** in the human body.

In an average lifetime, the **HUMAN HEART BEATS** more than

3 billion times.

A single **DROP OF BLOOD** contains **25,000 WHITE BLOOD CELLS.**

2—3 million **RED BLOOD CELLS** are created in the bone marrow **EVERY SECOND.**

SALIVARY GLANDS produce about **1—3.2 PINTS** (0.5–1.5 liters) of saliva **EVERY DAY.**

The liver has **MORE THAN 500 FUNCTIONS,** including **FILTERING BLOOD** and helping **DIGESTION.**

At rest, we breathe up to **20 times in a minute,** which adds up to **28,800 times in a day.**

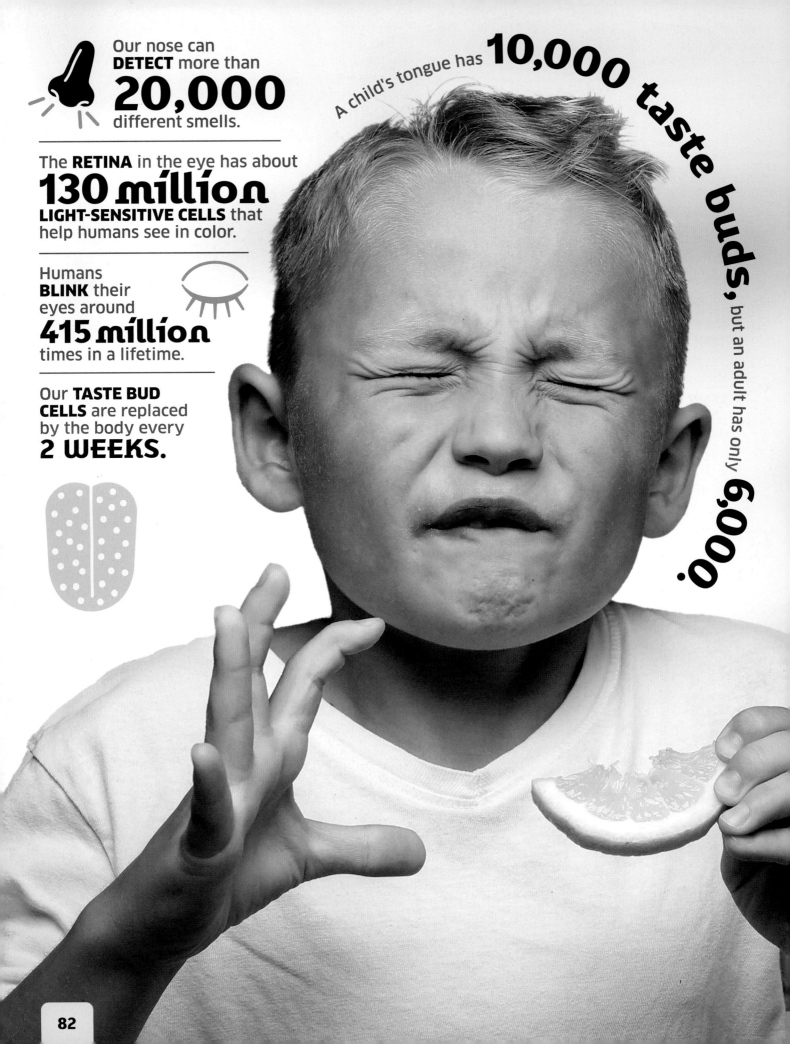

Our nose can **DETECT** more than **20,000** different smells.

The **RETINA** in the eye has about **130 million** **LIGHT-SENSITIVE CELLS** that help humans see in color.

Humans **BLINK** their eyes around **415 million** times in a lifetime.

Our **TASTE BUD CELLS** are replaced by the body every **2 WEEKS.**

A child's tongue has **10,000 taste buds,** but an adult has only **6,000.**

FINGERNAILS grow at an average rate of **⅛ IN** (3.47 mm) **PER MONTH**, while **TOENAILS** only grow **1/16 IN** (1.62 mm).

SKIN is the **LARGEST ORGAN** in the body and makes up **16%** of the body mass.

SENSES

The five main senses are taste, smell, hearing, sight, and touch. Sense organs such as your eyes, ears, and nose pick up the signals around you and send them to the brain, which in turn tells the body how to react.

2 PINTS (1 liter) of **MUCUS IS PRODUCED EVERY DAY** by the cells at the top of the **NOSE**.

THE TONGUE is made up of **8 MUSCLES** that help you speak and move food around when you eat.

A **FULL HEAD OF HAIR** contains more than **100,000 HAIRS**. Around **50—100** fall out each day.

Approximately **15,000 HAIR CELLS** in the ear help detect **SOUND**.

The **TONGUE** has about **200 MUSHROOM-SHAPED PAPILLAE** (tiny projections on the surface), each with up to **15 taste buds**.

The **HARDEST** substance in the body is the **TOOTH ENAMEL**. About **96%** of it is made up of the mineral **HYDROXYLAPATITE**.

Humans **SHED THE OUTER LAYER OF SKIN EVERY 2—4 weeks**. Over the course of a typical lifetime, this can amount to **77 LB** (35 kg) of **DEAD SKIN**.

The **EARDRUM** is a **THIN FILM** in the ear with a diameter of **⅜ IN** (9 mm) that **VIBRATES** when sound waves hit it.

Around **1 SQ IN** (6.5 sq cm) of **SKIN** can contain **650 SWEAT GLANDS, 20 BLOOD VESSELS**, and **1,000 NERVE ENDINGS**.

The **STIRRUP**, a tiny bone in the inner ear, is the **smallest bone** in the human body, measuring about **⅛ IN** (3 mm) **LONG**.

The human
BRAIN

Protected by your skull and linked to the rest of the body by a vast network of nerves, your brain controls your body's functions and movements as well as your thoughts, decisions, and memory.

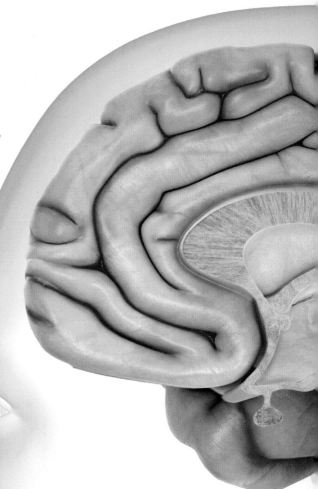

The **BRAIN FLOATS** in about
5 FL OZ
(150 ml) of **CEREBROSPINAL FLUID** that acts as a **SHOCK ABSORBER.**

A **SINGLE NEURON** (nerve cell) can have as many as
10,000
CONNECTIONS to other neurons.

At around 2.8—3 LB
(1.3–1.4 kg), your brain makes up about **2% OF YOUR BODY WEIGHT.**

A **HUMAN BRAIN** is **4 times HEAVIER** than the brain of our closest relative– the **CHIMPANZEE.**

The brain consists of **3 main parts:** the **CEREBRUM** controls actions, speech, and feelings; the **CEREBELLUM** coordinates movement and balance; and the **BRAIN STEM** controls reflexes.

THE HUMAN BRAIN contains around
200 BILLION
CELLS. Half of these are **NEURONS** that carry **ELECTRICAL SIGNALS** to other parts of the body.

There are more than

100 trillion synapses, or connections, between brain cells.

Hans Berger invented EEG
(electroencephalography)–a technique for measuring **ELECTRICAL ACTIVITY** in the brain using a machine.

The bundle of
fast-acting nerves
that form your spinal cord weigh about **1.2 oz** (35 g)–
THE SAME AS 3 AAA BATTERIES.

BLOOD, carrying oxygen and energy, flows through your **BRAIN'S BLOOD VESSELS** at a rate of
1.6 PINTS
(0.75 liters)
PER MINUTE.

About **20%** of the body's **OXYGEN SUPPLY** is used by the brain.

The brain itself **CANNOT FEEL PAIN** as it has
0 NOCICEPTORS
(pain-sensing receptors).

The width of a **SYNAPSE**–the connection between two neurons–is about
20–40 NANOMETERS
(billionths of a meter).

By the **AGE OF 3,** a **CHILD'S BRAIN** is
80%
the **SIZE OF AN ADULT'S.**

The **2 HEMISPHERES** (or halves) of the brain are joined by a band of
200–250 MILLION
nerve fibres called **THE CORPUS CALLOSUM.**

Stinky
POO AND GOO

Most creatures, including humans, produce a lot of waste products, such as poop, snot, and urine. As gross as these substances are, they all perform vital functions, such as getting rid of harmful bacteria and keeping the body healthy.

A giant heap of **BIRD AND BAT POOP** (known as **GUANO**), which was heavily mined in Peru in the 1800s, was more than **200 FT** (60 m) high–taller than the **LEANING TOWER OF PISA** in Italy.

A **MILKING COW** can produce between **26—50 GALLONS** (98–190 liters) of **SALIVA PER DAY.**

A **WOMBAT** can produce up to **100 CUBE-SHAPED POOPS** in a night. Some of the roughly ¾-IN- (2-cm-) square poops are used to **MARK THEIR TERRITORY.**

An **APHELORIA MILLIPEDE** secretes hydrogen cyanide that is **TOXIC ENOUGH TO KILL 18 PIGEONS or 6 MICE.**

PARROT FISH chew on coral and hard minerals and **POOP OUT** about **1,000 LB** (450 kg) of **SAND** each year.

FARTS, BURPS, and **POOP** from cows, pigs, sheep, and other livestock are responsible for about **14.5%** **OF GLOBAL GREENHOUSE GAS EMISSIONS.**

A **GIANT PANDA** poops about **40 TIMES A DAY.**

A human passes about **5,300 GALLONS** (20,000 liters) **OF GAS** in a lifetime–enough to fill **2,000 BALLOONS.**

On average, a **HUMAN POOP** contains **250 MICROSCOPIC PARTICLES OF PLASTIC.**

To protect itself against attack, a **PACIFIC HAGFISH** can create around **6 GALLONS** (24 liters) **OF SLIME.**

It can take a **SKUNK** up to **10 days** to replenish its **STINK SCENT** after spraying.

ABOUT 75% of a human poop is **WATER.**

An average **HUMAN POOP** has **210 calories** of energy—enough to charge **24 phones.**

Giraffes pick **GOOEY SNOT** from their nose with their **SLIMY, 20-IN- (50-cm-) LONG TONGUE.**

APOLLO ASTRONAUTS left **96 BAGS OF HUMAN POOP** on different parts of the **MOON.**

A COW produces about **80 GALLONS** (300 liters) of **METHANE** every day.

There are about **3,000 WASTE CHEMICALS** in **HUMAN PEE.**

The **CATERPILLAR** of a skipper butterfly can **SHOOT ITS POOP** about **5 FT** (1.5 m) away—a distance that is about **38 times its length.**

An **ELEPHANT** poops about **12—15 TIMES A DAY,** producing about **220 LB** (100 kg) of **DUNG.**

PEOPLE AND CULTURE

A world of PEOPLE

The population of the world has seen many changes in the past century, from birth rates to the free movement of people. More people than ever are moving to cities, and the difference in wealth between the rich and the poor is growing.

48% of **INTERNATIONAL MIGRANTS** in 2019 were **WOMEN.**

In 2020, **56.2%** of people around the world **LIVED IN CITIES.** That number is expected to **INCREASE** to **68%** by 2050.

250 YEARS AGO, the average life expectancy was **28.7 YEARS.** In 2019, that number rose to **72.6 YEARS.**

There were **140 million babies** born in 2020.

In **2017,** the **AVERAGE GLOBAL BIRTH RATE** was only **2.4 babies per woman,** compared to 4.7 in 1950.

More than **55 MILLION PEOPLE** visited Hong Kong in **2019.**

9.2% of people live **BELOW** the **GLOBAL POVERTY RATE**– meaning they live on **LESS THAN $1.90 A DAY.**

In 2018, the **WEALTH** of the world's **26 RICHEST PEOPLE** was equal to the wealth of the **POOREST 3,800,000,000.**

More than **800 MILLION PEOPLE** around the world **LACK ENOUGH FOOD** to meet their **BASIC NUTRITIONAL NEEDS.**

The **WORLD'S POPULATION** is expected to reach **9.7 BILLION** by **2050.**

79.5 MILLION people are **REFUGEES** who have been displaced from their home by **WAR, NATURAL DISASTERS, OR PERSECUTION.**

More than **272 MILLION** people–about **3.5%** of the world's population– live in a **DIFFERENT COUNTRY** than the one they were born in.

INDIGENOUS PEOPLES make up **5%** of the global population but **15% OF PEOPLE WHO LIVE IN poverty.**

In 2019, **141 million INTERNATIONAL MIGRANTS** lived in **EUROPE** or **NORTH AMERICA.**

In **2018,** people **UNDER THE AGE OF 18** made up **52%** of the global refugee population.

As of **2018,** there were more people **over the age of 65** than **under the age of 5.**

More people **travel** today than at any other point in history. There were **4.397 BILLION FLIGHT JOURNEYS** taken in 2019–more than **10 times more** than in 1975.

It was the **MOST-VISITED CITY** for **10 YEARS** from 2010–2019.

Earth's
CONTINENTS

The seven continents of the world are Africa, Asia, Europe, Australasia and Oceania, North America, South America, and Antarctica. Each continent is divided into countries, except for Antarctica, which doesn't belong to any one nation. The continents and their people vary greatly.

SOUTH AMERICA

82% of North Americans
live in **TOWNS** or **CITIES**, more than any other continent.

Just over **0.5%** of the world's people live in **OCEANIA**. With an area of **8 SQ MILES** (12 sq km), Nauru is **OCEANIA'S SMALLEST COUNTRY.**

More than **HALF** of the world's **POPULATION GROWTH** by 2050 is expected to occur in **Africa.**

About **THREE-FIFTHS** of the world's people live **IN ASIA.**

5 of the **10 SMALLEST COUNTRIES** in the world are found in **EUROPE:** Vatican City, Monaco, San Marino, Liechtenstein, and Malta.

Until **200 million years ago,** Earth's land was formed into one **SUPERCONTINENT** called **PANGAEA.**

8 out of the **10** countries with the **MOST AIRPORTS** are found in either **NORTH** or **SOUTH AMERICA.** The US has the most— **13,513.**

5 countries,
Russia, Turkey, Georgia, Kazakhstan, and Azerbaijan, are part of **2 CONTINENTS:** Europe and Asia.

Though the **290,600** people of **FRENCH GUIANA** live in **SOUTH AMERICA,** they are actually part of **FRANCE** and use the **EURO** as currency.

Modern humans, *HOMO SAPIENS,* evolved about **300,000 YEARS AGO** in **AFRICA.**

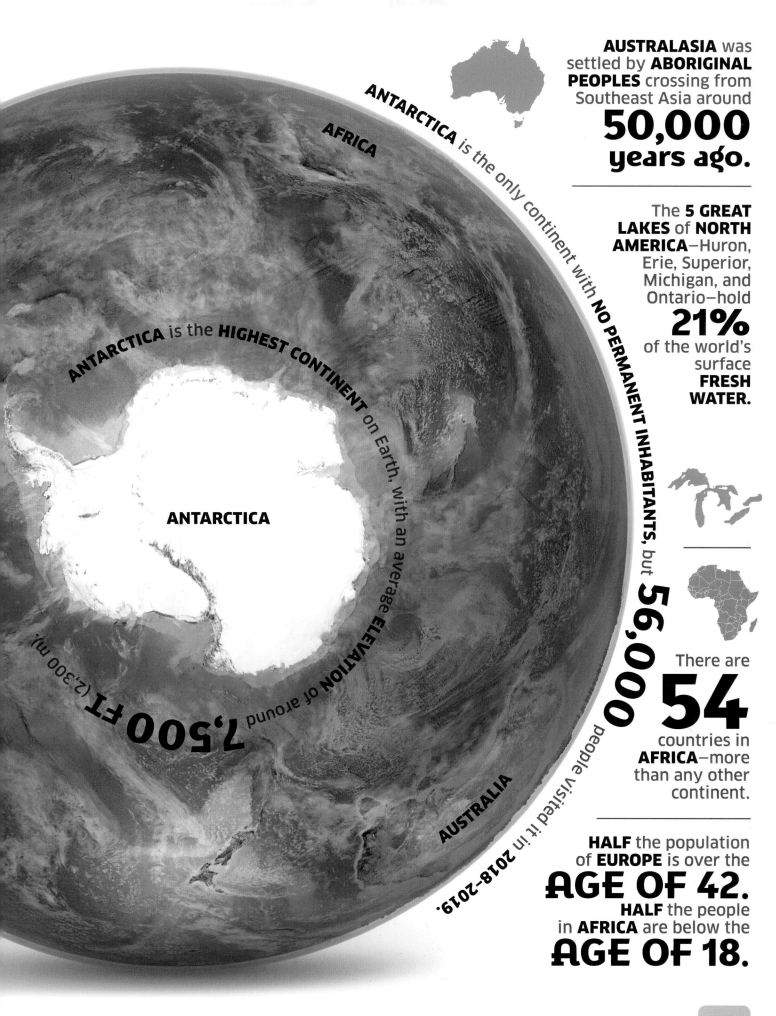

AUSTRALASIA was settled by **ABORIGINAL PEOPLES** crossing from Southeast Asia around **50,000 years ago.**

The **5 GREAT LAKES** of **NORTH AMERICA**—Huron, Erie, Superior, Michigan, and Ontario—hold **21%** of the world's surface **FRESH WATER.**

There are **54** countries in **AFRICA**—more than any other continent.

HALF the population of **EUROPE** is over the **AGE OF 42.** **HALF** the people in **AFRICA** are below the **AGE OF 18.**

ANTARCTICA is the only continent with **NO PERMANENT INHABITANTS,** but **56,000** people visited it in 2018–2019.

AFRICA

ANTARCTICA is the **HIGHEST CONTINENT** on Earth, with an average **ELEVATION** of around **7,500 FT (2,300 m).**

ANTARCTICA

AUSTRALIA

The world's COUNTRIES

From vast nations sweeping across continents to tiny inland states and groups of islands, countries are territories with their own governments. There are around 200 independent countries.

More than
1.4 BILLION PEOPLE
live in China, the country with the **LARGEST POPULATION** in the world.

With a highest point of just **7 FT 10 IN** (2.4 m), the **MALDIVES** is the **LOWEST-LYING COUNTRY.**

In **2011,**
SOUTH SUDAN became the world's **NEWEST COUNTRY** after **98.8%** of its voters opted for **INDEPENDENCE.**

49.8%
of all of **URUGUAY'S** population live in one city, **MONTEVIDEO.**

17 African countries,
including Cameroon, Togo, and Chad, became **INDEPENDENT** in **1960.**

VATICAN CITY is the world's **SMALLEST INDEPENDENT STATE.** At
0.17 SQ MILES
(0.44 sq km), it is more than
7 times smaller
than New York's Central Park.

ECUADOR and **CHILE** are the
only 2 SOUTH
AMERICAN NATIONS that don't share a **LAND BORDER** with **BRAZIL.**

With an area of **122 SQ MILES** (316 sq km), **MALTA** is the
smallest
member state of the **EUROPEAN UNION.**

MONGOLIA is the **LEAST DENSELY POPULATED NATION,** with an average of
2 PEOPLE
per **0.4 SQ MILES** (1 sq km).

325 international **land boundaries** separate the **WORLD'S NATIONS** and **DEPENDENCIES.**

INDIA is the world's **LARGEST DEMOCRACY. MORE THAN 900 MILLION PEOPLE** were eligible to vote in its **2019 GENERAL ELECTION.**

Roughly **17,500 ISLANDS** make up the nation of **INDONESIA.**

In **1893, NEW ZEALAND** became the first country to give **women the vote.**

SRI LANKA was the first country to be led by a **FEMALE** prime minister, **SIRIMAVO BANDARANAIKE,** in **1960.**

Mexico had **3 DIFFERENT** serving **PRESIDENTS** in **1 DAY** (February 19, 1913).

From **1988–1991,** the **BIGGEST BREAK-UP** of a single country saw the **Soviet Union** dissolve into **RUSSIA** and **14 OTHER STATES.**

In 2007, **SWITZERLAND** accidentally invaded **LIECHTENSTEIN** when **170 SWISS SOLDIERS** wandered **ACROSS THE BORDER** without realizing.

Canada and the US share the world's **LONGEST CONTINUOUS BORDER,** which is **5,525 MILES** (8,891 km).

There are over **50 million KANGAROOS** in Australia—**TWICE** the number of humans.

LIECHTENSTEIN, the **6TH** smallest country, is one of the world's leading exporters of **FALSE TEETH.**

RUSSIA, the **WORLD'S LARGEST COUNTRY,** spans **11 TIME ZONES.** When it's **7:00 AM** in Moscow, it's **4:00 PM** in the far east of the country.

Buzzing
CAPITALS

Almost every country has a capital city, which is often a central hub of government, trade, and culture. Some are small settlements, while others are the country's largest city.

There are more than

900
CHURCHES
in the **ITALIAN** capital of **ROME.**

The Nigerian capital city **ABUJA** is home to a **1,300-FT-** (400-m-) high monolith called **ASO ROCK.**

An average of
3,590,000
passengers per day travel through **SHINJUKU,** the world's **BUSIEST** railway station, in Japan's capital, **TOKYO.**

30°F
(–1.3°C) is the average annual temperature of **ULAANBAATAR, MONGOLIA**—one of the world's **COLDEST** capital cities.

Bangkok's
name contains
168 letters, which can be shortened to *Krung Thep* ("City of Angels").

FOR 13 YEARS,
between **1808** and **1821, RIO DE JANEIRO** in South America served as the capital of **PORTUGAL,** a country in **EUROPE.**

Located in **PARIS,** the capital of **FRANCE,** the **EIFFEL TOWER** receives about **7 MILLION VISITORS** every year.

From **1790–1800**, **PHILADELPHIA** served as the capital of the **US**, while **WASHINGTON, DC,** was being built.

At **459 FT** (140 m), **9 DE JULIO AVENUE** in **BUENOS AIRES, ARGENTINA,** is the **WIDEST** street in the world.

43 CE is the approximate year when **LONDON,** the capital of England, was established as **LONDINIUM** by the Romans.

BEIJING, the capital of **CHINA,** has **434.5 MILES** (699.3 km) of **TRAIN TRACKS** and **405 STATIONS.**

At a **LATITUDE** of **41 DEGREES SOUTH, WELLINGTON, NEW ZEALAND,** is the **southernmost** capital city in the world.

SOUTH AFRICA has **3 capital cities:** **PRETORIA** for the head of state, **CAPE TOWN** for law-making, and **BLOEMFONTEIN** for its courts.

Damascus, the capital of **SYRIA,** is one of the world's **OLDEST INHABITED CITIES.** People have been living there since **10,000 BCE.**

JAKARTA, the capital of **INDONESIA,** is home to **13 rivers** and is **SINKING** at an average rate of ⅜–6 IN (1–15 cm) per year.

Separated by the **CONGO RIVER,** the capital cities of **KINSHASA,** in the Democratic Republic of the Congo, and **BRAZZAVILLE,** in the Republic of the Congo, are less than **2.5 MILES** (4 km) apart.

39 MILLION is the projected population of India's capital **NEW DELHI** by 2030, which will make it the **MOST POPULOUS CITY** in the world.

TV WAS BANNED from being broadcast on **THURSDAYS** in **REYKJAVIK, ICELAND,** for **21 YEARS** (1966–1987).

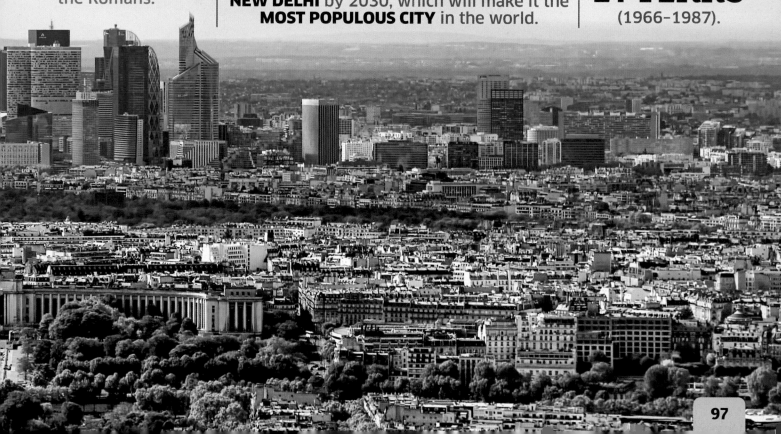

TOP 10
MOST POPULOUS WORLD CITIES

1 **TOKYO** • Japan • **37.34 MILLION**
A major political and economic center, Tokyo is the capital of Japan. In recent years, the birth rate has dropped and the influx of foreign workers has declined, which means Tokyo is expected to lose its top spot by 2030.

2 **DELHI** • India
31.18 MILLION
As well as a sprawling urban center, India's capital Delhi has a historic old town packed with Mughal architecture.

3 **SHANGHAI** • China
27.80 MILLION
Shanghai is known for its shining skyline of skyscrapers and as an important center for finance and business.

4 **SÃO PAULO** • Brazil
22.24 MILLION
Named after the Christian Saint Paul, São Paulo is a wealthy city, home to 111 different ethnic groups.

5 **MEXICO CITY** • Mexico
21.92 MILLION
Located in a valley in the Sierra Madre mountains, Mexico City is 7,350 ft (2,240 m) above sea level.

6 **DHAKA** • Bangladesh
21.74 MILLION
Several major rivers flow around densely populated Dhaka, which sits on the fertile Ganges Delta.

7 **CAIRO** • Egypt
21.32 MILLION
Filled with Islamic architecture and bustling bazaars, Cairo is also near Giza—the site of the Great Pyramid.

8 **BEIJING** • China
20.90 MILLION
Beijing's busy center holds both historical sites, such as the Forbidden City, and modern Olympic buildings from 2008.

9 **MUMBAI** • India
20.67 MILLION
Almost entirely surrounded by sea, Mumbai is the home of Bollywood—India's popular Hindi-language film industry.

10 **OSAKA** • Japan
19.11 MILLION
Osaka is nicknamed the "kitchen of Japan" due to its many wonderful culinary treats.

LANGUAGE

It's good to talk. Language lets us communicate and convey our ideas, emotions, and knowledge using sounds that form words. Over the years, individual languages have risen and fallen in popularity and sometimes have borrowed words from one another.

The United Nations has **6 official languages: ARABIC, CHINESE, ENGLISH, FRENCH, RUSSIAN, and SPANISH.**

ZIMBABWE has **16 official languages,** the most in the world.

517 LANGUAGES are spoken in **Nigeria,** more than any other **AFRICAN** country.

Around **two-fifths** of all the world's **LANGUAGES** are in danger of **DYING OUT.**

FRENCH is an official language in **29** countries.

There are **600,000 WORDS** in the **ENGLISH** language, more than **ANY OTHER LANGUAGE** in the world.

More than **HALF** of the world's population is **bilingual** —able to speak **2 LANGUAGES FLUENTLY.**

Around **80%** of all languages that are in use today are each spoken by **FEWER THAN 100,000 people.**

SILBO is a language that consists of **whistle sounds.** It has enabled people on **LA GOMERA** in the **CANARY ISLANDS,** off the coast of North Africa, to **COMMUNICATE** over distances up to **3 MILES** (5 km).

POPE FRANCIS, head of the Catholic Church, sends **TWITTER MESSAGES** in **9 LANGUAGES,** including Latin.

Despite his attempts to learn Dutch, when crowned ruler of Holland in **1806,** French **LOUIS BONAPARTE** declared himself **"RABBIT OF HOLLAND"** by saying **"KONIJN"** (rabbit) instead of **"KONING"** (king).

1,348,000,000
people speak **ENGLISH** as their **FIRST OR SECOND** language.

Less than 5% of **PORTUGUESE SPEAKERS** live in **PORTUGAL.** The majority, more than **200 MILLION,** are found **IN BRAZIL.**

The English word **"alphabet"** is derived from the **FIRST 2 LETTERS** of the **GREEK** alphabet— **ALPHA** and **BETA.**

Cristina Calderón, born in **1928,** is the **SOLE SURVIVING NATIVE SPEAKER** of the **YAGÁN LANGUAGE** from Tierra del Fuego (at South America's southernmost tip).

840 LANGUAGES
originate from or are spoken in **PAPUA NEW GUINEA,** more than any other country.

12.3% of the world's population speak **MANDARIN CHINESE** as their native language, making it the **MOST COMMON FIRST LANGUAGE** in the world.

In 2020, there were about **7,117 different languages** in use across the world.

Flying the
FLAG

Flags are flown by countries, regions, cities, and some organizations to identify, communicate, and commemorate. National flags are often powerful symbols, arousing pride and passion in their country's citizens.

The current US flag with **50 STARS** was designed by **17-YEAR-OLD** high school student **ROBERT HEFT** in **1958.**

Created more than **700 YEARS AGO,** the **DANISH NATIONAL FLAG,** or *Dannebrog*, is the oldest national flag in continuous use.

Since the **US NATIONAL FLAG** was adopted in **1777**, it has been modified **27 different times.**

THE WORLD'S TALLEST unsupported flagpole is in **JEDDAH.** It flies a Saudi Arabian flag and stands **561** FT (171 m) tall.

BELIZE'S FLAG has a wreath with **50 leaves** as a reminder of the year **1950**, when the country began a **31-YEAR QUEST** for independence.

The **SMALLEST FLAG** in the world is a Canada flag created in **2016**. It is **0.00004 IN** (0.001 mm) long or **1/100th** **THE WIDTH OF A HUMAN HAIR.**

THE ISLE OF MAN FLAG features **3 HUMAN LEGS** covered in armor, based on a symbol more than **600 YEARS OLD.**

Out of **195 countries' flags,** **85** have a width-to-length **ratio of 2:3.**

2 countries, **HAITI** and **LIECHTENSTEIN**, unknowingly arrived at the **1936 OLYMPICS** with **IDENTICAL NATIONAL FLAGS.**

32,823 ENTRIES were submitted to a 1901 **INTERNATIONAL COMPETITION** to design Australia's new flag.

The flag of **PIRATE BARTHOLOMEW "BLACK BART" ROBERTS** (1682–1722), who captured more than **400 ships,** depicted him standing on **2 HUMAN SKULLS.**

In a **2006 AUCTION, 4 FLAGS** from the American Revolutionary War (1775–1783) were sold for about

$17 million.

The **INDIAN FLAG** features a **24-spoke wheel,** called the **ASHOKA CHAKRA.** The spokes represent **PRINCIPLES OF BUDDHISM.**

PARAGUAY'S NATIONAL FLAG was changed

4 TIMES

in just **1 YEAR** (1811–1812).

Only **2 INDEPENDENT STATES** in the world fly **SQUARE FLAGS:** Switzerland and Vatican City.

World RELIGIONS

Religion is a set of beliefs that attempt to explain the purpose and meaning of life. Many people around the world follow different religions, each with their own beliefs and sacred rituals.

The Jewish holy book, the **TORAH**, has **613** *MITZVAHS*, or commandments.

70% of the world's people follow 1 of 3 religions– **CHRISTIANITY, HINDUISM, OR ISLAM.**

TAOISM is based on the teachings of **2 CHINESE PHILOSOPHERS–LAOZI AND ZHUANGZI.**

SHINTO developed as a religion in Japan around **2,000** years ago.

There are **10,600 verses** in the *RIGVEDA.*

The *RIGVEDA*, the **OLDEST-SURVIVING** sacred **HINDU** text, is approximately **3,500 YEARS OLD.**

Followers of **JAINISM** believe **24** spiritual leaders called **TIRTHANKARAS** appear in each **COSMIC CYCLE** of the universe.

One of the **YOUNGEST** large religions, the **BAHÁ'Í FAITH**, was founded in Persia (modern-day Iran) in **1844.**

48 copies of the Christian holy book, the Bible, were printed in **1455**, making it the **FIRST BOOK IN EUROPE** produced using a printing press.

The Cross Island Chapel in Oneida, New York, is the **WORLD'S SMALLEST CHRISTIAN CHURCH**, with only **2 SEATS.**

5 items starting with the letter **K** – **KACHERA** (a white undergarmen), **KANGHA** (a wooden comb), **KARA** (a steel bracelet), **KESH** (uncut hair), and **KIRPAN** (a short sword) – are worn by men who follow **SIKHISM.**

There are **114** *SURAS* (chapters) in the **KORAN**, the Islamic holy book. The longest has **286 VERSES** and the shortest has **3**.

Each year, more than **2 MILLION MUSLIMS** travel to **MECCA**, Saudi Arabia, to perform the pilgrimage called *HAJJ*.

The construction of the Roman Catholic Christian church **SAGRADA FAMÍLIA** in Barcelona is due to finish in **2026**– **144 years** after it began in **1882**.

A **7-BRANCHED MENORAH** (candle holder) is a symbol of **JUDAISM**. Each branch represents a day of the week.

Approximately **7%** of the world's population follow **Buddhism.**

ANGKOR WAT in Cambodia, the **LARGEST** religious structure in the world, was built in the **12TH CENTURY** as a **HINDU TEMPLE**. Less than **100 YEARS LATER**, it was converted to a **BUDDHIST TEMPLE**.

The founder of Buddhism, **SIDDHARTHA GAUTAMA**, is said to have meditated under a tree for **49 days** to obtain a state called **ENLIGHTENMENT**.

The diameter of the dome of the Muslim mosque **HAGIA SOPHIA** in Turkey is **108 FT** (33 m).

Around **83%** of all Sikhs live in **INDIA**.

TOP 10
TALLEST STATUES

1
STATUE OF UNITY • Gujarat, India
597 FT (182 m) • Completed **2018**
This statue of Vallabhbhai Patel, India's first deputy prime minister, is almost four times taller than the Statue of Liberty. Some 27,000 tons of steel and 77,000 tons of cement were used in its construction.

2
SPRING TEMPLE BUDDHA • Lushan, China
420 FT (128 m) • Completed **2008**
Made from 1,100 pieces of cast copper, the Spring Temple Buddha's estimated weight is 1,100 tons.

3
LAYKYUN SETKYAR • Monywa, Myanmar
116 FT (381 m) • Completed **2008**
Standing on a 44-ft- (13.5-m-) high throne in the village of Khatakan Taung, this statue of the Buddha took 12 years to build.

4
USHIKU DAIBUTSU • Ushiku, Japan
390 FT (120 m) • Completed **1993**
A 107,640-sq-ft (10,000-sq-m) garden surrounding the Ushiku Daibutsu Buddha is designed to be a Buddhist paradise.

5
SENDAI DAIKANNON • Sendai, Japan
328 FT (100 m) • Completed **1991**
Visitors to Sendai Daikannon can enter through the mouth of a carved white dragon at the statue's feet.

6
GUISHAN GUANYIN OF THE THOUSAND HANDS AND EYES
Changsha, China • **325 FT** (9 m) • Completed **2009**
A shining gilded-bronze sculpture, Guishan Guanyin depicts a Buddhist entity, known as a *bodhisattva*, who has 20 pairs of arms

7
GREAT BUDDHA OF THAILAND • Ang Thong, Thailand
302 FT (92 m) • Completed **2008**
It is said that those who touch the Great Buddha's right hand are blessed with luck.

8
DAI KANNON OF KITA NO MIYAKO PARK • Ashibetsu, Japan
289 FT (88 m) • Completed **1989**
With 20 floors inside, Dai Kannon houses several shrines and a viewing platform at the top.

9
RODINA-MAT' ZOVYOT! (The Motherland Calls)
Volgograd, Russia • **279 FT** (85 m) • Completed **1967**
The Motherland Calls depicts a woman thrusting a sword into the air and is the tallest statue outside of Asia.

10
AWAJI KANNON • Awaji Island, Japan
262 FT (80 m) • Completed **1982**
Meaning "World Peace Giant," Awaji Kannon was built by a local business man but is now falling into disrepair.

Italian artist **MICHELANGELO** painted more than

300 FIGURES

on the ceiling of **THE SISTINE CHAPEL** in Rome, after originally only being asked to paint **12**. It took him

4 years (1508–1512).

Japanese artist **YAYOI KUSAMA** first began painting her **"INFINITY NETS"**–vast canvases of polka dots–at the

**AGE OF
10.**

In **1998**, a **2.6-MILE-** (4.2-km-) tall image of an **INDIGENOUS AUSTRALIAN HUNTER**–called the **MARREE MAN**–was found carved in the ground in South Australia. The artist is **UNKNOWN**.

Anonymous street artist **BANKSY'S 13-FT-** (4-m-) wide painting depicting **BRITISH POLITICIANS AS CHIMPANZEES** was sold in **2019** for

£9,879,500.

In **2014**, a painting by US artist **GEORGIA O'KEEFFE** sold for

$44,405,000

–the **HIGHEST AMOUNT** ever paid for work by a female artist.

Italian artist **LEONARDO DA VINCI'S**

MONA LISA

measures just **30 X 21 IN** (77 x 53 cm) but has its **OWN ROOM** in the **LOUVRE MUSEUM** in Paris, France.

Astonishing
ART

From doodles to masterpieces, people have drawn, painted, sculpted, and crafted for thousands of years. The work of talented artists can entertain, inspire, and provoke powerful emotions.

An **OIL PAINTING** can take **2 weeks** to dry and harden.

Dutch painter **VINCENT VAN GOGH** produced around **2,000** sketches and paintings in his lifetime but did not gain popularity until **AFTER HIS DEATH** in 1890.

Ghanian artist El Anatsui's **GRAVITY AND GRACE** is a giant **37-FT-** (11.2-m-) long sheet made of more than

10,000 bottle caps.

In 1940, **4 TEENAGE BOYS** discovered caves in

Lascaux, France,

filled with **17,000-YEAR-OLD PAINTINGS**. Around

2,000 PREHISTORIC ANIMALS

decorate the walls, including stages, bison, and horses.

CALLIGRAPHY has been practiced as a major art form in China for more than **4,000 YEARS**. The **BASIC BRUSH OR PEN STROKES** are known as the **7 MYSTERIES.**

Japanese artist **Katsushika Hokusai** produced more than **30,000** works of art, including **THE GREAT WAVE OF KANAGAWA.**

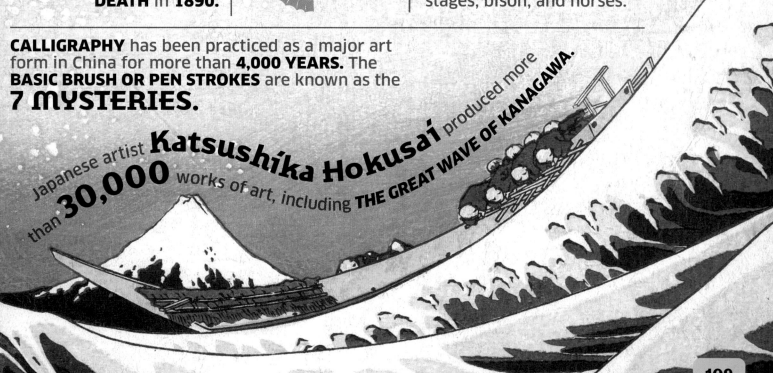

Listen to the
MUSIC

For thousands of years, many instruments have been made to beat out rhythms and play melodies. Today, a whole industry has grown up around music, with millions of recordings from a wide variety of artists sold each year.

A **PIANO KEYBOARD** has
88 KEYS,
52 white and **36** black.

An album needs to make
1,000,000
digital or physical sales to get a **PLATINUM CERTIFICATION** in the United States.

A traditional violin bow is made up of **150–200 HORSE TAIL HAIRS.**

VINYL RECORDS made up
26%
of all US album sales in **2019.**

Adolphe Sax invented and patented **14 different types of saxophone** in 1846–4 of which are in common use today.

DRAKE'S 2018 album *Scorpion* was streamed
132,450,203
times on Spotify on its **FIRST** day of release.

Vienna's **Vegetable Orchestra** has invented more than **150 INSTRUMENTS** from fresh produce, including **PUMPKIN DRUMS** and **LEEK VIOLINS.**

The **HIGHEST PIANO NOTE** – C8 – vibrates the air
4,186 times per second.

Some of the **OLDEST-KNOWN** musical instruments are **FLUTES** found in Germany, which were carved about

43,000
YEARS AGO.

Classical composer **WOLFGANG MOZART** completed his first symphony at the **AGE OF 8** and his first opera when he was

12 YEARS OLD.

The largest tambourine is **73 IN** (185.5 cm) in diameter and **14 IN** (36.5 cm) deep.

The **Royal Drummers of Burundi** use **3 TYPES OF DRUMS** in their performances - *Inkiranya, Amashako,* and *Ibishikiso.*

South Korean singer PSY's **"Gangnam Style"** was the first YouTube video to pass **1 billion views.**

A **CONCERT HARP,** also called the pedal harp, has up to

47 strings.

The **GREAT STALACPIPE ORGAN** in Luray Caverns, VA, produces tones by tapping

37 STALACTITES
of varying sizes with rubber-tipped mallets.

In 2019, the **GLOBAL RECORDING INDUSTRY** was worth

$20.2 BILLION.

A church in Germany began an **ORGAN PERFORMANCE** of John Cage's *As Slow As Possible* in 2001. It is set to last

639 YEARS.

On the STAGE

People have been going to the theater to watch plays for thousands of years. There are many different styles of performance, from Western theater, which can trace its origins back to Ancient Greece, to Chinese opera and Indian Kathakali (a form of dance).

A world record **6,952 tap dancers** performed a routine that was **135** seconds long, in Stuttgart, Germany, in **1998.**

The original production of the British musical **THE PHANTOM OF THE OPERA** had **130 CAST AND CREW, 22 SCENE CHANGES,** and **230 costumes.**

THE MOUSETRAP is the **LONGEST-RUNNING PLAY** in London's West End. The murder mystery has clocked **MORE THAN 28,000 PERFORMANCES** with more than **10,000,000 tickets** sold since 1952.

There are **101 CLASSICAL STORIES** in **KATHAKALI,** a form of storytelling through dance that originated in South India in the **17th century.**

8 TONY AWARDS were given to US composer **STEPHEN SONDHEIM— THE MOST** ever won by a **COMPOSER.**

In **1987,** Adrian Hilton recited the complete works of **WILLIAM SHAKESPEARE** in **110 hours, 46 minutes.**

There are **368** styles of **Chinese opera.** Only around **280** are still performed today.

MARGARET HUGHES played Desdemona from *OTHELLO* in 1660. She was the **FIRST PROFESSIONAL ACTRESS** to appear in a Shakespeare play, **44 years** after his death.

In **493 BCE,** Greek playwright, Phrynichus was fined **1,000 DRACHMAS** (equal to 2 years' income for a farmer) because his play **THE CAPTURE OF MILETUS** made the audience cry.

In **1964,** ballet stars **RUDOLF NUREYEV** and **MARGOT FONTEYN** made a record **89 CURTAIN CALLS** after performing **SWAN LAKE** in Vienna, Austria.

Tap dancer **ANTHONY MORIGERATO** managed **1,163 TAPS PER MINUTE** (19.4 per second) at a New York dance school in **2011.**

The Lion King is the BIGGEST-GROSSING MUSICAL –earning **$9.1 billion** by the end of 2019.

In 2018, the **WORLD'S LARGEST BALLET LESSON,** involving **1,530 students,** took place in Hong Kong, China.

The Ancient Greek open-air theater at **EPIDAURUS** could seat up to **14,000 PEOPLE.**

Rodgers and Hammerstein's *SOUTH PACIFIC* has won **17 TONY THEATER AWARDS,** more than any other musical.

At the MOVIES

In 1895, an audience of 30 enjoyed the first moving pictures show at the Grand Café in Paris, France. Millions now flock to their local theater every week to enjoy the latest films.

INDIA is the **LARGEST PRODUCER OF MOVIES** in the world, creating more than

1,200 FILMS EVERY YEAR.

AN OSCAR STATUETTE STANDS

13½ IN

(34 cm) high, weighs **8.5 LB** (3.9 kb), and is made of bronze plated in **24-carat gold.**

In **1928,** Mickey Mouse made his official debut in the **8-MINUTE MOVIE** *Steamboat Willie.*

722 FT

(220 m) is the **LONGEST BUNGEE DROP IN A MOVIE,** made by stunt man Wayne Michaels from a **SWISS HYDRO-ELECTRIC DAM** for the James Bond movie *GoldenEye* (1995).

US actress Rebecca Romijn spent

8—9 HOURS

in make-up a day and wore **ALMOST 100 PROSTHESES,** or fake body parts, for the role of Mystique in the original *X-MEN* movie (2000).

With just **18 SEATS** and an area of **258 SQ FT** (24 sq m), **CABIRIA CINE-CAFÉ** in Brasilia, Brazil, is the **smallest PURPOSE-BUILT CINEMA IN THE WORLD.**

It costs an average of

$100 MILLION

to create and market a **MAJOR STUDIO MOVIE.**

More than **300,000 extras** appeared in the funeral scene of the movie *GANDHI* (1986).

TOY STORY (1995) was the first feature-length, computer-animated movie. The film had **114,240 FRAMES** and each took **45 minutes to 30 hours** to render on computer.

The first movies that were made were **SILENT.** In **1927,** the first **TALKIES**—movies with **SYNCHRONIZED SOUND AND IMAGES**—appeared in theaters.

The world's **LARGEST** permanent 35-mm movie screen is in Suzhou, China, and measures about **3.5 TIMES** the area of **A TENNIS COURT.** 113 FT 6 IN x 87 FT 10 IN (34.6 x 26.8 m)–

Hong Kong actor **Jackie Chan** has the **HIGHEST NUMBER OF CREDITS** in a single movie– **15 TIMES** in *Chinese Zodiac* (2012).

In 2005, an **ORIGINAL POSTER** of the German movie *METROPOLIS* (1927) sold for **$690,000.**

American actress Tatum O'Neal was just **10 YEARS OLD** when she won the **1974 BEST SUPPORTING ACTRESS OSCAR** for her role in *Paper Moon* (1973).

Animators had to draw **2.3 MILLION individual hairs** to create Sulley from *MONSTERS, INC.* A single frame took an average of **12 hours** to complete.

In 2020, *Parasite*, directed by **2-TIME OSCAR WINNER** Bong Joon-Ho, became the **first foreign language film** to win the Oscar for **BEST PICTURE.**

19,000 COSTUMES, 48,000 pieces OF ARMOR, and **MORE THAN 1,800 PAIRS** of hobbit feet and ears were produced for the Lord of the Rings trilogy (2001–2003).

40 SQUIRRELS were trained to **SORT NUTS** on a conveyor belt for *CHARLIE AND THE CHOCOLATE FACTORY* (2005).

TERRY, the **DOG** who played Toto in *The Wizard of Oz* (1939), was paid **$125 A WEEK,** which was **MORE MONEY** than some of the **HUMAN ACTORS** received.

The calls of **5 different animals** (bear, walrus, lion, seal, and badger) were blended together to create **CHEWBACCA'S VOICE** in the **STAR WARS** film series.

SOLO SPORTS

Many sports, such as tennis and wrestling, pit an individual against a single opponent, while in sports such as cycling and athletics, athletes race against each other for the top prize. Solo sports are often a test of power, accuracy, and strategy.

According to the rules of darts, the **BULL'S EYE** (center) of a dartboard must be **½ IN** (12.7 mm) across and **5 FT 8 IN** (1.73 m) high.

A Formula One driver can **LOSE** up to **8.8 LB** (4 kg) **IN WEIGHT** during a **GRAND PRIX RACE.**

Gymnasts perform impressive jumps, leaps, and turns on a **BALANCE BEAM** that is just

4 IN (10 cm) wide.

3 different weapons are used in fencing—**ÉPÉE, FOIL, and SABER.**

A TABLE TENNIS BALL weighs just **0.09 OZ** (2.7 g) and is the **LIGHTEST** ball of any sport.

A game of **SNOOKER** is played with **22 balls** of **8 DIFFERENT COLOURS,** including the white cue ball.

Between **1981** and **1986,** Pakistan's **JAHANGIR KHAN** won an impressive **555 CONSECUTIVE** squash games.

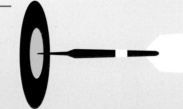

In croquet, the **HOOPS** are only about 1⁄16 — 3⁄16 IN (0.15–0.45 cm) **WIDER THAN THE BALLS.**

Between **1977** and **1987**, US athlete Edwin Moses won **122** consecutive **400M HURDLES RACES**— the longest-ever **WINNING STREAK** in track and field.

When officials lost count during the **3,000-M STEEPLECHASE** final at the **1932 OLYMPICS**, the athletes had to run an **extra lap.**

At the **1904** Olympics, US gymnast George Eyser won **6 medals** while wearing a **PROSTHETIC WOODEN LEG.**

The **LONGEST TENNIS MATCH** ever played was at Wimbledon, UK, in 2010, between John Isner and Nicolas Mahut—**183 GAMES** over **11 hours, 5 minutes.**

During **SHORT-TRACK SPEED-SKATING RACES**, skaters can reach speeds of up to **28 MPH** (45 km/h).

A traditional badminton **SHUTTLECOCK** is made up of **16 GOOSE FEATHERS** fitted into a cork base and weighs only about **0.18 oz** (5 g).

The most **SUCCESSFUL PARALYMPIAN** is US swimmer Trischa Zorn, with **41** gold, **9** silver, and **5** bronze medals.

More than **54,250 balls** a year are stored at **68°F** (20°C) before being used in the UK's **WIMBLEDON** tennis championships.

In 2012, **12-YEAR-OLD** Tom Schaar became the **FIRST PERSON** to perform a **1080**, or **3** full revolutions on a **skateboard.**

The fastest men's **TENNIS SERVE** was **163.7 MPH** (263.4 km/h), made by Australian Sam Groth in **2012.** Spanish player Georgina Garcia Pérez set the women's record, **136.7 MPH** (220 km/h), in 2018.

At the **1912** Olympics, a single Greco-Roman wrestling bout lasted **11 HOURS, 40 MINUTES.** Today, bouts are staged over **2 x 3-MINUTE** rounds.

During the **1928 OLYMPICS SCULLS COMPETITION,** Australian rower Bobby Pearce stopped to let a **LINE OF DUCKS** pass. He still won the race by **29 seconds.**

Playing as a
TEAM

Many of the most popular sports are played by teams who compete against each other. The number of players on a team varies from sport to sport—from four in curling to 18 in Australian rules football.

The Philadelphia Warriors' Wilt Chamberlain scored a record **100 POINTS** in **49 MINUTES** of a single **NBA BASKETBALL GAME** in 1962.

Each **MAJOR LEAGUE BASEBALL** team plays **162 GAMES** in a regular season—that's a total of

2,430

MLB games per year.

VOLLEYBALL was invented in

1895

and was originally called "Mintonette."

Russian **ICE HOCKEY** player Denis Kulyash's

110.3–MPH

(177.5-km/h) **SHOT** in 2011 is the fastest in history.

Spain made **779 PASSES**, an average of **8.5 PER MINUTE**, in their **2018 FIFA WORLD CUP** football match against Russia.

5-A-SIDE and **9-A-SIDE** versions of **NETBALL** existed before **7-A-SIDE TEAMS** became the **STANDARD** in 1960.

There are

108 double stitches

on an MLB baseball, which are **HAND SEWN** using **88 IN** (223.5 cm) of waxed red thread.

In a game of **OCTOPUSH,** a form of underwater hockey,

6 PLAYERS

on each side propel a

2.6–3.3 LB

(1.2-1.5 kg) **PUCK** along the pool floor.

Each **STONE** used in the game of **CURLING** weighs just under

44 LB (20 kg).

In **1939**, South Africa and England scored a collective

1,981 runs

over a period of

12 DAYS

—the longest recorded **CRICKET TEST MATCH.**

Japanese rugby player **DAISUKE OHATA** holds the world record for test tries— **69 IN 58 MATCHES.**

2 teams based in the **ISLES OF SCILLY** make the world's smallest soccer league, playing **18 LEAGUE MATCHES** as well as **2 CUP COMPETITIONS.**

The fastest-recorded **LACROSSE SHOT** was made by American Patrick Luehrsen at **119.9 MPH** (192.96 km/h), in Illinois in 2015.

Brazil's Cristiane Rozeira scored **3 goals** in their match against Jamaica during the 2019 WOMEN'S FOOTBALL WORLD CUP.

In **WATER POLO,** each team is allowed to hold onto the ball for up to **30 SECONDS** before shooting at the goal.

The **SLOVAKIAN WOMEN'S ICE HOCKEY TEAM** averaged a goal **every 44 seconds,** defeating Bulgaria **82–0** during the 2008 Olympics.

In 2006, a **TRANSFER FEE** of **33 LB** (15 kg) of **SAUSAGES WAS PAID** for Romanian soccer player Marius Cioara.

119

TOP 10 OLYMPIANS

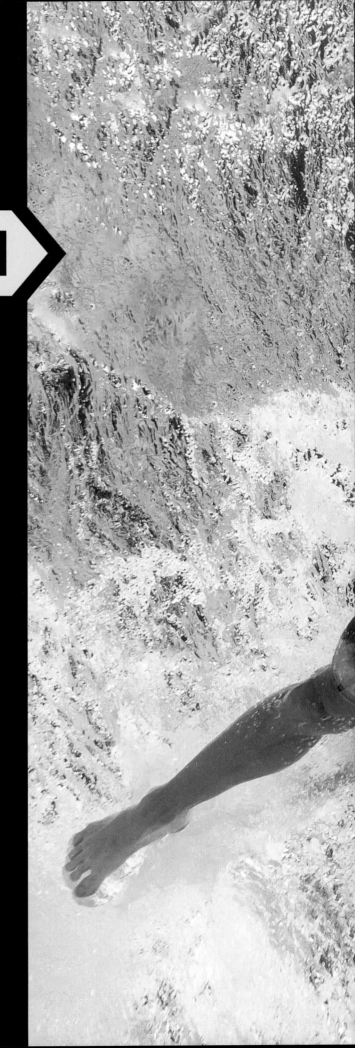

MICHAEL PHELPS • USA
Swimming • **28** (**23** gold, **3** silver, **2** bronze)

1

The most decorated Olympian of all time, Michael Phelps also set a world record when he won eight gold medals at the 2008 Olympics in Beijing, China.

2 **LARISA LATYNINA** • Soviet Union
Gymnastics • **18** (**9** gold, **5** silver, **4** bronze)

Larisa Latynina holds the record for the most gold medals won by a gymnast, male or female.

3 **MARIT BJØRGEN** • Norway
Cross-country skiing • **15** (**8** gold, **4** silver, **3** bronze)

A five-time Olympian, Marit Bjørgen is the most decorated Winter Sports Olympian in history.

4 **NIKOLAI ANDRIANOV** • Soviet Union
Gymnastics • **15** (**8** gold, **4** silver, **3** bronze)

In the 1976 Montreal games, Nikolai Andrianov earned medals in 7 out of 8 possible events, including 4 golds.

5 **OLE EINAR BJØRNDALEN** • Norway
Biathlon • **13** (**8** gold, **4** silver, **1** bronze)

Biathlete Ole Einer Bjørndalen used to train for 900–1,000 hours every year, until he retired in 2018.

6 **BORIS SHAKHLIN** • Soviet Union
Gymnastics • **13** (**7** gold, **4** silver, **2** bronze)

Specializing in the pommel horse, Boris Shakhlin was the most successful athlete at the 1960 Summer Olympics.

7 **EDOARDO MANGIAROTTI** • Italy
Fencing • **13** (**6** gold, **5** silver, **2** bronze)

Winning his first gold medal at just 17, Edoardo Mangiarotti is Italy's most decorated Olympian ever.

8 **TAKASHI ONO** • Japan
Gymnastics • **13** (**5** gold, **4** silver, **4** bronze)

Takashi Ono was inducted into the International Gymnastics Hall of Fame in 1998.

9 **PAAVO NURMI** • Finland
Track athletics • **12** (**9** gold, **3** silver)

In 1924, Paavo Nurmi became the first athlete ever to win five gold medals at a single Olympic Games.

10 **BIRGIT FISCHER** • East Germany/Germany
Canoeing • **12** (**8** gold, **4** silver)

Kayaking champion Birgit Fischer is the only woman to win Olympic medals 20 years apart.

10 **BJØRN DÆHLIE** • Norway
Cross-country skiing • **12** (**8** gold, **4** silver)

Nicknamed "Rocketman," Bjørn Dæhlie has the most medals of any cross-country skiier in Olympic history.

The written
WORD

Words enable new ideas, stories, and instructions to be shared with others. They can be published in a variety of formats, from poetry and books to newspapers and online magazines.

PAPER
was first made by a Chinese court official in **105 BCE.**

British author **MARY SHELLEY** was just **19 YEARS OLD** when she completed *Frankenstein* in **1817**–one of the first **SCIENCE FICTION** novels.

US businessman Bill Gates paid **$30,802,500** for Leonardo da Vinci's **72-PAGE CODEX LEICESTER**– making it the world's **MOST EXPENSIVE BOOK.**

US author Theodor Geisel, known as **Dr. Seuss,** used just **50 DIFFERENT WORDS** in his 225-word book *Green Eggs and Ham* in order to win a **$50 bet** with his publisher.

Indian author Vickrant Mahajan signed **6,904 COPIES** of his book *YES THANK YOU UNIVERSE* in **2016,** setting a record for the **MOST BOOKS SIGNED** in a single session.

A Tokyo bookshop, Morioka Shoten in Ginza, sells copies of **ONLY 1 TITLE EACH WEEK.**

In a Japanese **haiku poem, 17 syllables** are arranged across **3 LINES** with **5, 7,** and **5 SYLLABLES,** respectively.

In **1901**, British writer **BEATRIX POTTER** printed just

250 COPIES

of *The Tale of Peter Rabbit*, which has since gone on to sell more than

45,000,000 COPIES.

There are

5 LINES

in a **LIMERICK POEM.** Usually, the **1ST, 2ND,** and **5TH** lines all rhyme.

The world's smallest book, *Teeny Ted from Turnip Town*, measures **0.003 IN** by **0.004 IN** (0.07 mm by 0.10 mm) and has **30 TINY PAGES** that can only be read using a **POWERFUL SCANNING ELECTRON MICROSCOPE.**

86% of adults around the world today can **READ AND WRITE,** compared to **42%** in **1960.**

The **US LIBRARY OF CONGRESS** adds around

10,000 new items

to its collection every day.

A traveling **CAMEL LIBRARY** in Ethiopia uses

21 camels

to transport

200 books

to children in **33 ISOLATED VILLAGES.**

The Sumerian **EPIC OF GILGAMESH** was recorded on **CLAY TABLETS** nearly

4,000 YEARS AGO.

3,000 copies

of the world's **SMALLEST NEWSPAPER** were printed in Portugal in 2012. Each copy weighed only **0.04 OZ** (1 g).

More than

500 million

copies of the **HARRY POTTER BOOKS** have sold worldwide. **STACKED IN A LINE** next to each other, they could **WRAP AROUND THE GLOBE** more than

16 TIMES.

The longest **line of books** ever measured was **20,142.42 FT** (6,139.41 m).

Tasty
FOOD

Humans need food to live, but we don't just eat to survive. From cheesy pizzas to delicious desserts, people have learned how to prepare thousands of dishes to make eating a pleasure.

Made in **2012**, the world's **LARGEST PIZZA** covered an area of **13,580.28 SQ FT** (1,261.65 sq m)—about **2.5 TIMES** the size of a basketball court.

The **DURIAN FRUIT** is so **SMELLY** that any passengers taking one on the Singapore Metro System face a fine of **$500** (SGD).

It takes around **140,000** crushed cochineal insects to make **2 LB** (1 kg) of **E120 red dye,** which is used to color some jams, sweets, and many other foods.

In **2019,** the town of Chécy in France served the largest **FRUIT SALAD,** weighing **22,796 LB** (10,340 kg).

About **660 GALLONS** (2,500 liters) of **WATER** are used to grow **2 LB** (1 kg) **of rice.**

THE LONGEST CARROT EVER grown was **20 FT 6 IN** (6.25 m) long.

In **2019, LA CASA GELATO** in Vancouver, Canada, broke records by offering **238 flavors OF GELATO** (a type of ice cream), including curry, roasted garlic, and chocolate bacon.

Around **3,500** cooks and **21,870** waiters prepared and served dishes to **22,295** people at the Banquet of Mayors held in Paris, France, in **1900**.

The world record for **MOST TOMATOES** grown on a single plant is **1,355,** achieved by retired farmer Surjit Singh Kainth in the UK in **2013**.

It takes about **2.6 GALLONS** (10 liters) of **COW'S MILK** to make **2 LB** (1 kg) of cheese.

106,420,000,000 servings of **INSTANT NOODLES** were enjoyed around the world in **2019**.

The oldest-known **COOKBOOK** is about **3,700 YEARS OLD.** It is a collection of **25 RECIPES FOR STEW** recorded on **3 MESOPOTAMIAN CLAY TABLETS**.

The Finnish restaurant **KUAPPI** is the **SMALLEST** restaurant in the world—with space for only **1 TABLE FOR 2 DINERS**.

WHITE TRUFFLES are the most expensive edible **FUNGI**, often costing **£3,000 PER KG.**

14% of all food is **WASTED** between when it's harvested and when it goes on sale.

Nearly **46,000,000 TURKEYS** are consumed in the United States at **THANKSGIVING DAY DINNERS**.

Up to **500** auk seabirds are sewn into seal skin and left for **3–18 months** to make **KIVIAK**, a dish from Greenland.

165,000 saffron crocus **FLOWERS** are needed to get **2 LB** (1 kg) of **SAFFRON SPICE**.

2 TORTOISES
became the **FIRST CREATURES** to orbit **THE MOON**, on board the 1968 space probe, **ZOND 5.**

A CAT'S SKELETON contains
244 bones,
38 more than an adult human.

Brandy, a boxer, had the
LONGEST DOG TONGUE,
measured at **17 IN** (43 cm)–the length of
2 SMALL DOGS.

There are only **3,900 TIGERS** left in the **WILD** but more than
5,000
tigers kept as pets in the US.

In **2019, ITALIANS** kept
12,880,000
pet birds,
more than any other country in Europe.

CATS can detect **SOUNDS** more than **3 TIMES HIGHER** than those humans can hear.

NALA, a rescue cat, has **4.3 MILLION** followers on Instagram.

GUNTHER IV, a **GERMAN SHEPHERD,** has a personal fortune of **$375 MILLION** due to his father inheriting the entire fortune of German countess Karlotta Liebenstein in **1992.**

All about
PETS

For thousands of years, people have kept pets of all shapes and sizes for entertainment and companionship. Dogs may have been the first pets, but hundreds of different creatures have made it into people's homes ever since.

Many people believe **GOLDFISH** only have a **3-SECOND MEMORY,** but experiments have proved they can remember information for **5 months.**

In **1989,** Zorba, an Old English Mastiff, broke his former record for the **HEAVIEST DOG,** weighing **343 LB** (155.6 kg)—heavier than **2 ADULT HUMANS.**

There are **24 SPECIES** of **HAMSTER,** but **ONLY 5** are commonly kept as pets.

39 IN (99.5 cm) is the **HIGHEST JUMP** by a rabbit, a record set in 1997.

In 2011, kelpie dog Abbie Girl surfed a **305-FT 8-IN** (107.2-m) **WAVE** near San Diego, California.

Budgerigar Puck could say **1,728 DIFFERENT WORDS**—the most of any bird.

BUDGERIGARS are covered in up to **3,000** feathers.

€21 BILLION was spent on **PET FOOD** in Europe in 2019.

RABBITS' TEETH never stop growing. They grow about **4¾ IN** (12 cm) a year.

Russia is home to **22.8 million** pet cats.

Around **2.2 MILLION REPTILES** are kept as pets in **FRANCE,** more than in any other EU nation.

HISTORY

Ancient
EGYPT

Founded on the banks of the Nile River, ancient Egypt was the world's greatest civilization for almost 3,000 years. It was ruled by a succession of pharaohs (kings or queens), who were believed to be links between the people and the gods.

The **ANCIENT EGYPTIANS** worshipped more than **2,000 different gods and deities.**

The ancient Egyptian **WEEK** lasted **10 DAYS.**

The **EGYPTIAN** *mummification* **process** for preserving **DEAD BODIES** took around **70 DAYS.**

ANCIENT EGYPTIAN FARMERS observed **3 seasons,** which centered around farming: **AKHET** (flooding season), **PERET** (growing season), and **SHEMU** (harvest season).

11 PHARAOHS took the name **RAMSES** or **RAMESSES,** meaning "BORN OF THE SUN-GOD, RA."

Cats were sacred to the **CAT GOD BASTET** and often mummified. One **TOMB** held more than **80,000 CAT MUMMIES.**

TUTANKHAMUN was just **8** or **9** years old when he became **PHARAOH.** He died when he was **19.**

Egyptians believed a person's **STOMACH, LIVER, INTESTINES, AND LUNGS** would be needed in the **AFTERLIFE.** During mummification, they were **TAKEN OUT** and **STORED** in **4 CANOPIC JARS.**

The **Great Sphinx** in Giza is a statue of a mythological creature with a **HUMAN HEAD** and a **LION'S BODY.** It is **240 FT** (73 m) long and **66 FT** (20 m) tall.

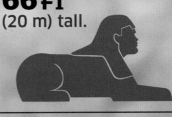

Tutankhamun was buried in **3 COFFINS NESTED WITHIN EACH OTHER.** The innermost coffin was made of gold and weighed **243 LB** (110 kg).

Hieroglyphics, the Egyptian writing system, was made up of about **700** different **PICTURE SYMBOLS.**

An ancient **EGYPTIAN MEDICAL TEXT** includes about **700 spells and remedies.**

This gilded wooden guardian statue was among the **5,000 objects** discovered in the tomb of the young pharaoh **Tutankhamun.**

ONE OF THE LARGEST STONE STRUCTURES on Earth, the
GREAT PYRAMID
covers an area equal to about
200 tennis courts.

Among **TUTANKHAMUN'S TOMB POSSESSIONS** was a chariot,
130
walking sticks, a trunk of boomerangs, and
2
trumpets.

Circus Maximus, a chariot-racing stadium in Rome, was **1,864 FT** (568 m) long and could seat as many as **250,000 spectators.**

The **ROMANS** constructed more than **250,000 MILES** (400,000 km) of **ROADS,** out of which **50,000 MILES** (80,000 km) were **PAVED.**

The **BIGGEST ROMAN GALLEYS** were **180 FT** (55 m) long, could carry **120 soldiers,** and were powered by **300 oarsmen.**

In Roman mythology, **CERBERUS** was a **3-HEADED DOG** that guarded the entrance to the **UNDERWORLD.**

Roman foot soldiers were called legionaries. **8 LEGIONARIES** formed a unit called a contubernium. **10 CONTUBERNIA** made up a century. **6 CENTURIES** usually made up a cohort. **10 COHORTS** made up a legion.

The **WESTERN HALF** of the Roman Empire fell to **GERMANIC TRIBES** in **476 CE,** but the **EASTERN EMPIRE** ruled for another **977 YEARS.**

A LEGION of Roman soldiers was made up of about **6,000** men.

According to legend, Rome was **FOUNDED** in **753** BCE by twin brothers **ROMULUS AND REMUS**, who were raised by a **SHE-WOLF**.

Ancient ROME

With the forces of a mighty army, the ancient Romans built a vast empire, from Britain in the north to Egypt in the south. At its fullest extent in the 2nd century CE, it stretched 2,500 miles (4,000 km) from east to west.

ROME is believed to be the first city in the world to have **1,000,000** inhabitants.

Between **193** and **476 CE**, **32** of the **59** **ROMAN EMPERORS** were murdered while in office.

Julius Caesar added **EXTRA DAYS** to the year **46** BCE, making it last **445 DAYS** to bring the new calendar in line with the **SOLAR YEAR**.

At its largest, the **ROMAN EMPIRE WAS HOME TO** a population of **65 million** people.

A Roman legionary could **MARCH** up to **18.5 MILES** (30 km) a day, carrying a sword, spear, and clothing weighing up to **88** LB (40 kg).

The giant **CARACALLA PUBLIC BATHS** in Rome had **50 FURNACES** that burned more than **8.8 TONS** of wood a day.

The **COLOSSEUM** in Rome opened in **80 CE** with **100 days** of games.

The **3** greatest **ROMAN GODS** were **JUPITER**, ruler of the heavens, **JUNO**, goddess of women, and **MINERVA**, goddess of wisdom.

Imperial
CHINA

China was made up of many warring kingdoms until it was united by the First Emperor Qin Shi Huang in 221 BCE. The empire lasted almost 2,000 years, until revolution forced the Last Emperor to abdicate in 1912.

Built in **210–209 BCE**, the **TOMB** of Emperor Qin Shi Huang lay buried for **2,180 YEARS** before it was found in **1974** by farmers digging a well.

Parts of the **Great Wall** reach **26 FT** (8 m) high and **24.5 FT** (7.5 m) thick.

EMPEROR QIANLONG (1711–1799 CE) is believed to have written more than **42,000 POEMS** during his lifetime.

The **13-STORY-HIGH** Iron Pagoda in Kaifeng city has survived **38 EARTHQUAKES, HAIL, WINDSTORMS,** and **16 FLOODS** since it was built in **1049 CE.**

WU ZETIAN—the only **FEMALE EMPEROR** in China's history— ruled for **15 years,** from **690–705 CE.**

Admiral Zheng He led **7 GREAT VOYAGES.** The first, in **1405,** included **62** huge **"TREASURE SHIPS"** and **27,800 MEN** and reached Vietnam, India, and Sri Lanka.

IN 1908, PUYI became the **LAST EMPEROR** of China at **THE AGE OF 2.**

The **GREAT WALL OF CHINA** was built between the **3rd** century BCE and the **17th** century CE. The total current length of the system is **13,170 MILES** (21,196 km).

Spanning **1,115 MILES** (1,794 km), the Grand Canal, or Jing–Hang Grand Canal, is the **LONGEST HUMAN-MADE WATERWAY IN THE WORLD.**

GUNPOWDER, then called black powder, was **INVENTED** in China in the **9TH CENTURY CE** by mixing **3 INGREDIENTS:** charcoal, sulfur, and saltpeter (potassium nitrate).

THE FORBIDDEN CITY palace complex in Beijing spans an area of **7,800,000 SQ FT** (720,000 sq m), which is about **9.5 times** bigger than **BUCKINGHAM PALACE** in London.

Between 742–1100 CE, China's **POPULATION DOUBLED** to more than **100 MILLION PEOPLE,** making it the most populous country in the world.

Commissioned in **1403** to document traditional Chinese knowledge, the **YONGLE ENCYCLOPEDIA** was completed in 1408 and contained **22,877 CHAPTERS** across **11,095 VOLUMES.**

Paper was invented in China, 1,000 YEARS before it was made in Europe.

Built by more than **1,000,000 workers, THE FORBIDDEN CITY** contains **980 BUILDINGS** surrounded by a **170-FT-** (52-m-) wide **MOAT.**

Qing Dynasty emperor **KANGXI** ruled for **61 YEARS** (1661–1722 CE), the **LONGEST** of any Chinese emperor.

Found in Emperor Qin Shi Huang's burial chamber, the **TERRACOTTA ARMY** includes more than **8,000 LIFE-SIZE CLAY SOLDIERS, HORSES, AND CHARIOTS.**

The Aztecs used
CACAO BEANS
(also known as cocoa) as **CURRENCY.**
A rabbit would cost about
10 cacao beans,
AND A MULE ABOUT 50.

Founded in **1325, TENOCHTITLAN**—capital of the Aztec empire—covered an area of
5 SQ MILES
(13 sq km).

In **1521**, Spanish conquistadors **LAY SIEGE** to Tenochtitlan for **117 DAYS, DESTROYING** much of the city before the Aztecs surrendered.

The **TEMPLE** at the center of Tenochtitlan, used for **SACRIFICES TO THE GODS**, was **240 FT** (60 m) high, or the height of **14 DOUBLE-DECKER BUSES.**

The Aztecs **counted in 20s.** They used dots and lines to show numbers from **1** to **19** and a **FLAG SHAPE** for **20.** They used a **FEATHER** for the number **400.**

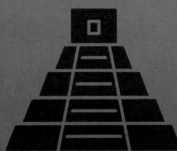

The **AZTECS** believed in more than
200 GODS AND GODDESSES.

In **1500**, the **POPULATION** of Tenochtitlan was about **200,000**—more than **3 TIMES** that of London at the time.

This **CEREMONIAL MASK** of **XIUHTECUHTLI**, the **Aztec god of fire**, is made of **THOUSANDS** of pieces of **TURQUOISE** and **7 SHELL TEETH.**

AZTECS AND INCAS

In the 14th and 15th centuries, the Aztec Empire flourished in Central America, while the Inca Empire extended 2,500 miles (4,000 km) along the Andes mountains. Both great cultures were destroyed by the arrival of Spanish soldiers from 1521.

At its greatest extent in the **1520s,**
THE INCA EMPIRE
covered approximately
770,000 SQ MILES
(2,000,000 sq km)—more than **8 TIMES THE SIZE OF THE UK.**

Built in the mid-15th century, **Machu Picchu** is a huge Inca citadel containing about **200 BUILDINGS** and more than **3,000 STONE STEPS.**

At its peak, the **INCA EMPIRE'S** population was close to **12 million.**

To connect their **VAST TERRITORY,** the **INCA** built more than **24,000 MILES** (39,000 km) **of roads.**

Around **80%** of **INDIGENOUS PEOPLE DIED** from **DISEASES** brought over **FROM EUROPE,** such as smallpox, to which they had **NO IMMUNITY.**

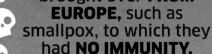

Fortresses and CASTLES

Across the world, strongholds and citadels of stone, brick, or wood have been built high in the landscape to protect settlements and their surrounding territory from attack. They were also the homes of important people, such as kings, queens, and nobles.

Since 1707, **BEARS** have been kept in the moat surrounding the almost **800-YEAR-OLD ČESKÝ KRUMLOV CASTLE** in the Czech Republic.

MOSZNA CASTLE in Poland boasts **365 ROOMS** and **99 TURRETS.**

ALNWICK CASTLE in northern England has appeared in **41 TV SHOWS AND FILMS,** including as **HOGWARTS CASTLE** in the first **2 HARRY POTTER MOVIES.**

HARLECH CASTLE in Wales was **BESIEGED** for **7 YEARS** (1461–1468) before its force of **50 MEN** surrendered to King Edward IV's **army of 10,000.**

The Japanese **TEMPLE FORT** of Ishiyama Hongan-ji defended itself **AGAINST A SIEGE** for **10 YEARS** (1570–1580).

Completed in **1679,** the 5-sided **CASTLE OF GOOD HOPE** in South Africa has a **BELL** for sounding the **ALARM** that can be heard up to **6 MILES** (10 km) **away.**

In **1920,** during renovations of **BRAN CASTLE** in Romania, a **532-YEAR-OLD FORGOTTEN SECRET PASSAGEWAY** was discovered behind a fireplace.

Windsor Castle has been home to the **BRITISH ROYAL FAMILY** for more than **950 YEARS.** It has more than **1,000 ROOMS** and **300 FIREPLACES.**

CHITTORGARH FORT in INDIA had **84 WELLS OR RESERVOIRS,** holding up to **1,057,000,000 GALLONS** (4,000,000,000 liters) **OF WATER,** enabling its inhabitants to withstand **LONG SIEGES.**

MORE THAN 16,000,000 BRICKS

were used to build **FORT JEFFERSON** in the Florida Keys. Although under construction for **30 YEARS,** the fort was **NEVER COMPLETED,** or **ARMED.**

THE LARGEST CASTLE IN THE WORLD

is **MALBORK CASTLE** in **POLAND.** This 13th-century castle is spread across **52 ACRES** (21 hectares) and once was home to around **3,000 KNIGHTS.**

Predjama Castle

in Slovenia is built out of a **9-MILE-** (14-km-) long **CAVE** halfway up a **403-FT-** (123-m-) high **CLIFF.**

At **22.4 MILES** (36 km) long and **16 FT 6 IN** (5 m) thick, **KUMBHALGARH FORT** has the world's **LONGEST FORT WALLS.**

23 SIEGE ATTEMPTS have been made on **EDINBURGH CASTLE,** Scotland. The **SHORTEST** in 1639 saw the castle taken in **30 minutes.**

There are more than

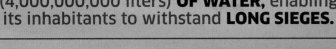

2,400

SANSEONG— ancient mountain fortress sites— in **KOREA.**

Japan's **Himeji Castle** has more than 80 BUILDINGS and a 151-FT- (46-m-) tall fortress.

In the **15TH CENTURY,** despite lacking the wheel, cranes, or iron tools, the **INCA OF PERU** cut and transported stone blocks, more than **110 TONS** each, to build the fortress of **Sacsayhuaman.**

In **1869,** work began on **NEUSCHWANSTEIN CASTLE** in Germany—the first castle to include **MODERN CENTRAL HEATING, TELEPHONES, AND AN ELECTRICITY GENERATOR.**

In the **8th century,** the early Islamic states formed one of the world's **LARGEST EMPIRES,** stretching **5,000 MILES** (8,000 km).

Starting in **610,** the **KORAN,** the holy book of Islam, was **revealed to the Prophet Muhammad** through the Archangel Gabriel over a **PERIOD OF 22 YEARS.** There are **114 CHAPTERS** in the Koran.

Al-Zahrawi wrote the **MEDICAL ENCYCLOPEDIA** *AL-TASRĪF* (*The Method*) around the **YEAR 1000.** It had **30 volumes** and included drawings and descriptions of **200 DIFFERENT SURGICAL INSTRUMENTS.**

The **OTTOMAN EMPIRE** began in Turkey in 1299 and lasted for **623 years.**

In **1453,** Sultan **MEHMED II** **conquered the city of Constantinople** after a **SIEGE** lasting **55 DAYS.** It came to be known as Istanbul and became the capital of the **Ottoman Empire.**

The **LIBRARY** of the **UMAYYAD CALIPHS** of Córdoba, Spain, had more than **400,000 books.**

In 1590, Shah Abbas I shifted **THE CAPITAL OF THE SAFAVID EMPIRE** to Isfahan, today in Iran. The city had **162 MOSQUES, 48 SCHOOLS,** and more than **250 PUBLIC BATHS.**

The **SULTAN AHMED MOSQUE** has **9 domes** and is surrounded by **6 minarets.**

SULTAN AHMED MOSQUE in Istanbul is also known as the **BLUE MOSQUE** after the more than **20,000 TURQUOISE BLUE TILES** that decorate its interior.

The Ottomans' **DARDANELLES GUN**, a giant cannon made in 1464, weighed **18.5 TONS** and could **FIRE STONE BALLS** of up to **25 IN** (63 cm) in **DIAMETER**.

ISMAIL I was just **14 YEARS OLD** when he was declared shah (king) of Persia (modern-day Iran) in 1501, starting a **NEW RULING DYNASTY–the Safavids.**

SULTAN MURAD II gave up his throne in **1444**, appointing his son **MEHMED II, WHO WAS** **12** **YEARS OLD,** as the new ruler.

The **CRESCENT MOON AND STAR** was used as a symbol by the Turks in the 15th century and has become the symbol of Islam. **THE FIVE-POINTED STAR** reflects the 5 obligations of Islam, known as the **Five Pillars.**

The longest-serving Ottoman sultan, **SULEIMAN THE MAGNIFICENT,** reigned for **45 YEARS, 11 MONTHS.** His death in **1566** was kept a secret from his soldiers for **48 DAYS.**

The world of
ISLAM

From the 7th Century onward, Islam spread through the Middle East and into parts of Europe, Africa, and Asia. Islamic armies conquered new lands and empires grew, in which science, art, and architecture flourished.

After coming to power in 1595, **MEHMED III** had all **19** of his **BROTHERS** **EXECUTED** so they could not overthrow him.

Some 900 gardeners tended the greenery in the **12 GARDENS** surrounding the **Topkapi Palace,** the **MAIN RESIDENCE** of the Ottoman rulers in modern-day Istanbul.

36 SULTANS ruled the Ottoman Empire, starting with **OSMAN I** and ending with **MEHMED VI.**

Medieval kingdoms of
AFRICA

Africa has been home to numerous powerful kingdoms and empires throughout its long history. By building and expanding trade routes, many kingdoms in medieval Africa expanded their wealth and influence across large parts of the continent and beyond.

A **9-FT-** (2.7-m-) tall statue in Baghaï, Algeria, commemorates **DIHYA**, a **warrior queen** of the indigenous Amazigh people who **FOUGHT AND DEFEATED** an invading Arab army in the **7TH CENTURY.**

In medieval times, caravans of camels would carry **BLOCKS OF SALT** weighing **200 LB** (90 kg) across the Sahara.

Approximately **1 million stones** were used to build the **GREAT ENCLOSURE** in the city of Great Zimbabwe.

MANSA MUSA, ruler of the **MALI EMPIRE** from 1312–1337, is said to be the **RICHEST MAN EVER.** His **FORTUNE,** from trade in **GOLD AND SALT,** would be about

$400 billion.

On his **PILGRIMAGE TO MECCA** in 1324, Mansa Musa's caravan included **60,000 MEN** and about **80 CAMELS,** each loaded with up to

300 LB
(136 kg) of **GOLD.**

Following **SONNI ALI'S** reign from **1464–1492,** the **SONGHAI KINGDOM** grew to cover more than **1,400,000 SQ KM** (540,000 sq miles)

In the **15th** century, **SANKORÉ UNIVERSITY** in Timbuktu, in modern-day Mali, had **25,000 STUDENTS.**

Each of the Djenné Great Mosque's **3 TOWERS** is topped with an **OSTRICH EGG,** symbolizing **fertility.**

The **16—24-in-** (40–60-cm-) thick **WALLS** of the Great Mosque at Djenné, Mali, are built of **blocks of river mud.**

With **400,000–700,000** books, Sankoré University library had the **BIGGEST COLLECTION OF WRITINGS** in Africa in the **14th–15th centuries.**

18 bronze heads were found in Nigeria in **1938**. They were made by the **Yoruba people of Ife** from the **12TH–15TH CENTURIES,** and depicted **kings** and other important figures.

OBA OZOLUA (1483–1514), the second of the **5 GREAT WARRIOR KINGS** of the Benin Empire, is said to have **WON 200 BATTLES.**

According to legend, **Askía the Great (1443–1538)** handed out around **100,000 PIECES OF GOLD** to the poor while on his **PILGRIMAGE TO MECCA.**

Completed **AROUND 1460, THE KINGDOM OF BENIN** was defended by **10,000 MILES** (16,000 km) of earth barriers.

TOP 10 LONGEST-REIGNING MONARCHS

1 **LOUIS XIV** • France
72 YEARS • 1643–1715

Born in 1638, Louis XIV was only four years old when he succeeded his father, Louis XIII, as king of France. Also known as the Sun King, he ruled an absolute monarchy, where he held supreme authority with unlimited power.

2 **BHUMIBOL ADULYADEJ** • Thailand
70 YEARS • 1946–2016

A popular modern king, Bhumibol was served by 30 prime ministers before he died at the age of 88.

3 **PRINCE JOHANN II** • Liechtenstein
70 YEARS • 1858–1929

Johann was a quiet ruler who loved art. He became known as "Johann the Good" due to his support of worthy causes.

4 **QUEEN ELIZABETH II** • United Kingdom and Commonwealth
69 YEARS • 1952–Present

The longest-reigning monarch alive today, Elizabeth presides over not only the UK but 15 other Commonwealth realms.

5 **K'INICH JANAAB' PAKAL** • Mayan kingdom of Palenque
68 YEARS • 615–683 CE

Assuming the throne at the age of 12, Pakal ruled over the city of Palenque in modern-day Mexico and expanded its influence.

6 **FRANZ JOSEPH I** • Austria (from 1848) and king of Hungary (from 1867) • **67 YEARS** • 1848–1916

During his reign, Franz Joseph was involved in major political events in Europe, including the start of World War I.

7 **CONSTANTINE VIII** • Byzantine Empire (co-ruler)
66 YEARS • 962–1028 CE

Mostly ruling jointly with other relatives, Constantine was sole emperor for just three years at the end of his life.

8 **RAMSES II** • Ancient Egypt
66 YEARS • 1279–1213 BCE

Known as Ramses the Great, he commissioned more monuments than any other Egyptian ruler, including the great temple at Abu Simbel.

9 **BASIL II** • Byzantine Empire (co-ruler)
65 YEARS • 960–1025 CE

An effective military and administrative leader, Basil ruled during the golden age of the Byzantine Empire.

10 **FERDINAND I OF THE TWO SICILIES** • Kingdom of Sicily
65 YEARS • 1759–1825

Ferdinand governed two kingdoms—Naples and Sicily. During his reign, he faced war, revolution, and uprisings.

This list covers rulers of independent states only. King Pepi II of ancient Egypt is excluded because the dates attributed to his reign are under debate.

Changing FASHIONS

From corsets to clogs and belts to breeches, clothing through the ages has been weird and wonderful as well as practical and protective. Fashion has allowed people to express their identities, convey status in society, and even fight for their country.

A medieval suit of metal **PLATE ARMOR** weighed **60—70 LB** (25–30 kg), about the weight of **2 GOLD BARS.**

Popular in the 14th and 15th centuries, the **POINTED ENDS** of **CRAKOW SHOES** could extend as far as **9½ IN** (24 cm) past the toes.

French queen **MARIE ANTOINETTE** (1755–1783) had **300 DRESSES** made for her **PER YEAR.**

European 15th-century steeple-shaped **HENNIN HATS** were about **3 FT 3 IN** (1 m) tall.

In Imperial Rome, **TOGAS** were formed of semicircular lengths of cloth around **18 FT** (5.5 m) long and up to **9 FT** (2.75 m) wide.

In **1873, JACOB W. DAVIS** and **LEVI STRAUSS** patented the classic **BLUE DENIM JEAN,** as workwear for **MINERS.** The **FIRST PAIR** sold for **$6** worth of **GOLD DUST.**

5,000 years ago, elite Egyptians **SHAVED THEIR HEADS AND WORE WIGS** to protect them from the sun and head lice.

Popular in **16TH-CENTURY VENICE,** some women's platform shoes, called **CHOPINES,** were **20 IN** (50 cm) tall. This protected their dresses from **MUD** and was a **DISPLAY OF STATUS.**

Giant skirts called **CRINOLINES,** supported by a **CAGE OF HOOPS** and fashionable in Europe in the **EARLY 1860S,** were up to **18 FT** (5.5 m) in diameter.

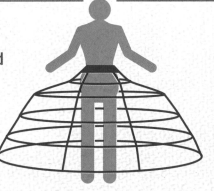

IRENE SPARKS from New Zealand owned **21,321 TIES** —the **LARGEST COLLECTION** ever recorded.

In **1946**, French designer Louis Réard invented the **BIKINI** using only **0.22 SQ FT** (0.02 sq m) of fabric.

In 2018, **4.5 BILLION PAIRS OF JEANS** were sold **WORLDWIDE.**

Severe cotton shortages during **WORLD WAR I** saw some German soldiers' **UNIFORMS** made with **15% COTTON** and **85%** fibers from **STINGING NETTLES.**

First appearing around the **8TH CENTURY,** a Japanese noblewoman's **JŪNIHITOE** had **12 SEPARATE KIMONOS,** or clothing layers.

From **1747–1782,** a British law made wearing a **KILT** or other traditional Scottish clothing punishable by **6 months' IMPRISONMENT.**

HIGH HEELS
were first worn by **PERSIAN HORSEMEN** in the **10TH CENTURY.**

About **1 IN** (2.5 cm) tall, they helped **KEEP THEIR BOOTS IN THE STIRRUPS.**

Ruffs were **NECK COLLARS** worn in 16th-century Europe—the biggest were **12 IN** (30 cm) **WIDE** and had up to **600 PLEATS.**

147

Into
BATTLE

Throughout the ages, people have taken arms to settle disputes or conquer new lands. Some battles, including many in the two World Wars of the 20th century, changed history.

SCYTHED CHARIOTS with **3-FT 3-IN-** (1-m-) long **METAL BLADES** fitted to their wheels were first used in India and Persia around **2,500 YEARS AGO.**

ARROWS from the bows of 13th-century **MONGOL WARRIORS** could hit targets **1,050 FT** (320 m) away.

JOAN OF ARC was **17 YEARS OLD** when in 1429 she led the **FRENCH ARMY** to relieve the city of Orleans, which was **BESIEGED** by the English.

According to legend, a **MESSENGER RAN 25 MILES** (40 km) to announce the Athenian defeat of the Persians after the **Battle of Marathon in 490 BCE.**

More than **400 boats** were **DESTROYED** by the use of a hand-pumped **FLAMETHROWER** during the **919 CE** Battle of Langshan Jiang between **RIVAL CHINESE KINGDOMS.**

Norman invaders from northern France, including **2,000–3,000 CAVALRY,** defeated English forces in **1066** to **conquer the country.**

During the **1422 SIEGE OF KARLŠTEJN CASTLE** (in present-day Czech Republic), attackers used a catapult to fire **2,000 wagon loads of animal dung** over the castle walls.

 In **1916, the first tanks,** the British Mark I, entered **COMBAT** at the Battle of Flers-Courcelette in **WORLD WAR I.**

As many as **12,000 war elephants** served in the armies of the **MUGHAL EMPEROR** Jahangir (1569–1627). They were covered in **350 LB** (159 kg) of **IRON PLATE ARMOR** and carried soldiers into battle.

The first **AIRCRAFT BOMBING RAID** was in **1911,** when an Italian pilot dropped **4 LARGE GRENADES** in Libya.

At its peak in 1813, French Emperor **NAPOLEON BONAPARTE** had an army of around **1 MILLION SOLDIERS.**

About **35,000 MILES** (56,000 km) of **TRENCHES** were dug in Europe's **WESTERN FRONT** during World War I, enough to encircle Earth **1.4 TIMES.**

6 German U-boat submarines sank **274 SHIPS** between them during **WWII.**

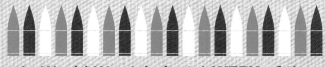 In World War I, in just **1 WEEK** of the **BATTLE OF THE SOMME,** the Allies fired **AROUND 1,500,000 ARTILLERY SHELLS.**

It is estimated that **300 MILLION SOLDIERS** saw combat in **WORLD WAR II** (1939–1945).

SCIENCE AND TECHNOLOGY

Essential
ELEMENTS

An element is a substance that is made up of just one type of atom. From gases in the atmosphere to metals in mobile phones, elements make up everything in the Universe.

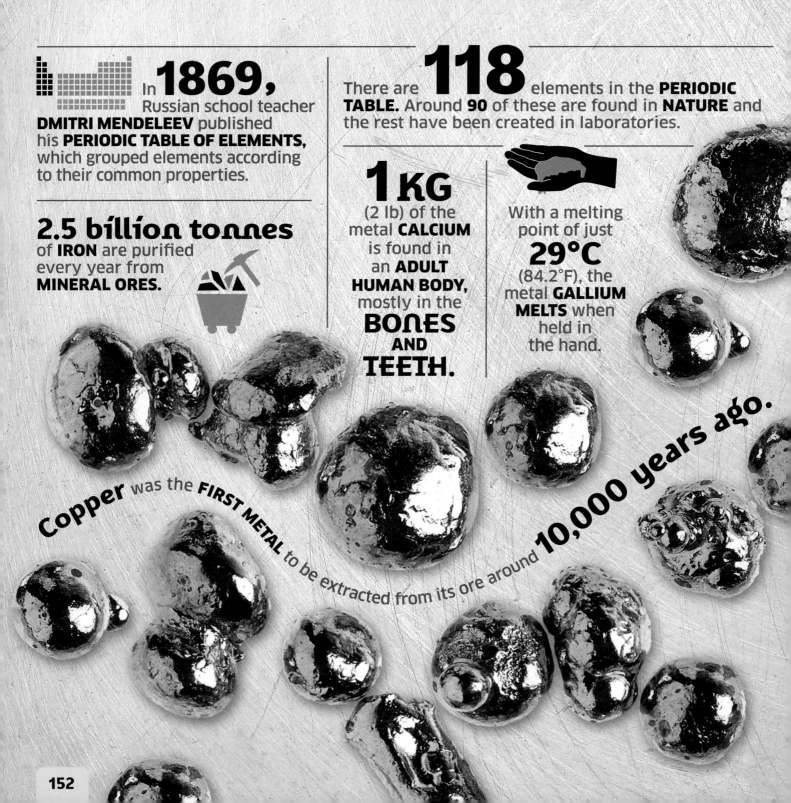

In **1869,** Russian school teacher **DMITRI MENDELEEV** published his **PERIODIC TABLE OF ELEMENTS,** which grouped elements according to their common properties.

2.5 billion tonnes of **IRON** are purified every year from **MINERAL ORES.**

There are **118** elements in the **PERIODIC TABLE.** Around **90** of these are found in **NATURE** and the rest have been created in laboratories.

1 KG (2 lb) of the metal **CALCIUM** is found in an **ADULT HUMAN BODY,** mostly in the **BONES AND TEETH.**

With a melting point of just **29°C** (84.2°F), the metal **GALLIUM MELTS** when held in the hand.

Copper was the **FIRST METAL** to be extracted from its ore around **10,000 years ago.**

3,41'°C
(6,177°F) **IS THE MELTING POINT OF TUNGSTEN.** It is the **HIGHEST MELTING POINT** of all the metals.

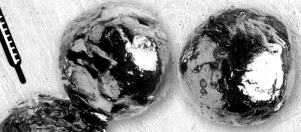

OXYGEN
makes up
21%
of **EARTH'S ATMOSPHERE.**

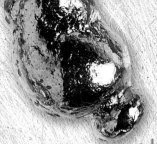

In **1937**, *technetium* became the first element to be **ARTIFICIALLY PRODUCED** in a laboratory.

 90% of minerals found in Earth's crust contain **SILICON** – the element used in **ELECTRONIC CIRCUITS.**

10 million
different **COMPOUNDS** (a combination of 2 or more elements) can be formed using **CARBON** – more than any other element.

About
99%
of the **HUMAN BODY** is made up of **6 ELEMENTS –** 65% OXYGEN, 18.5% CARBON, 10% HYDROGEN, 3% NITROGEN, 1.5% CALCIUM, AND 1% PHOSPHORUS. The other 1% is made up of traces of lots of other elements.

Only **2 ELEMENTS** exist in **LIQUID FORM** at room temperature – **MERCURY** and **BROMINE.**

HENNIG BRAND became the first person to discover **PHOSPHORUS** in 1669 when he boiled and filtered **50 BUCKETS OF URINE.**

WELCOME STRANGER
is the largest nugget of **PURE GOLD** ever found. It was discovered in Australia in 1869, and weighed
66 KG
(145.5 lb).

NITROGEN
gas turns into a **CLEAR, COLOURLESS LIQUID** when cooled to below
–195°C
(–319°F). It is used as a **COOLANT** to freeze different types of food, such as **ICE CREAM.**

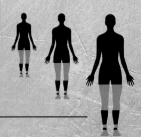

RECYCLING 1 ALUMINIUM CAN
saves enough energy to run a TV for **3 HOURS.**

Neon is one of the **RAREST ELEMENTS ON EARTH.** This gas makes up only
0.001% of our atmosphere.

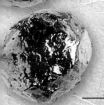

Sound and LIGHT

Light and sound are both forms of energy that travel as waves. They can be refracted (bent), reflected, and detected by your senses. Light moves faster than sound and can pass through a vacuum, such as space, while sound needs to travel through something to be detected.

 It takes **8 minutes, 19 seconds** for light to travel from the **SUN TO EARTH.**

A **LIGHT-YEAR** is the distance it takes light to travel in a year through a vacuum, which is about **5.9 TRILLION MILES** (9.5 trillion km).

SUNLIGHT shining through **RAINDROPS** in the air can form a **RAINBOW.** The longest-lasting rainbow was observed in Taiwan, China, for **8 HOURS AND 58 MINUTES.**

IN A VACUUM, light travels at the speed of **186,000 MILES** (300,000 km) per second.

The **SPEED OF LIGHT** slows down to **124,000 MILES** (200,000 km) per second in **WATER.**

Sound's intensity (loudness) is measured in **DECIBELS** (dB). At **188 dB,** the call of a **BLUE WHALE** can be louder than a **JET PLANE.**

In 1947, **CHUCK YEAGER** became the **FIRST PERSON** to travel faster than the speed of sound— **757 MPH** (1,235 km/h)— aboard the Bell X-1 rocket plane.

 **PITCH** (how high or low a sound is) is measured in hertz (Hz). The normal range of **HUMAN HEARING** is **20 to 20,000 Hz.**

CATS can detect **HIGH-PITCHED SOUNDS** of **64,000 Hz.**

AURORAS—colorful light displays in Earth's atmosphere—occur up to **620 MILES** (1,000 km) high.

It would take about **7 YEARS** to walk the distance of **1 LIGHT SECOND,** assuming a constant speed of **3 MPH** (4.8 km/h).

The **OLDEST** recorded sound is a **20-SECOND** excerpt of the song **"AU CLAIR DE LA LUNE"** recorded by a device called a phonautograph in **1860.**

Shortly after the **BIG BANG,** the universe **WENT DARK**—there was no light for at least **100 MILLION YEARS.** This period is known as the **COSMIC DARK AGES.**

About **10—35%** of people have **PHOTIC SNEEZE REFLEX,** in which emerging into bright light causes **SNEEZING.**

About **90%** of the creatures living in the open ocean below **1,640 FT** (500 m) are **BIOLUMINESCENT** (organisms that produce light).

Sound travels more quickly through denser substances. In **WATER** it travels at the speed of **4,921 FT** (1,500 m) per second, which is **4.4 times** faster than through air.

For a human brain to detect an **ECHO,** the **MINIMUM TIME** between a sound and its reflection must be **1/10th OF A SECOND.**

More than **75% of the energy** we use to **POWER OUR HOMES** comes from nonrenewable fuels, such as **COAL, OIL,** and **NATURAL GAS.**

In 2015, **ICELAND** was completely powered by renewable energy sources— **73% hydropower** and **27% geothermal energy.**

A candle emits around **80 WATTS OF ENERGY** a second.

Only **10% OF electricity** that passes through an incandescent light bulb filament is **CONVERTED INTO LIGHT**—the rest is lost as heat energy.

At the bottom of a **ROLLER COASTER HILL,** your body weight **TRIPLES** due to gravitational force.

There are more than **31 MILLION JOULES** of energy in **0.26 GALLONS** (1 liter) of gas.

About **10 million billion** coal-burning power stations would be needed to generate as much energy as the **SUN.**

HEAT ENERGY is measured in **CALORIES** (cal). It takes **1 CAL** to raise the temperature of **0.04 OZ (1 g)** of **WATER** by **1.8°F** (1°C).

The engines of the **SATURN V ROCKET**—used to launch missions to the Moon—could generate **34.5 million NEWTONS OF THRUST** at lift-off, around **288 TIMES** more than that produced by a **COMMERCIAL JET AIRCRAFT.**

FORCES are measured in **newtons** (N). You can grip with a force of around **300N.**

ENERGY AND FORCES

Energy is what makes things work—from a burning flame to a rocket blasting off into space. Many different types of energy exist, including chemical, electrical, kinetic, and thermal. Forces are needed to transfer energy from one type to another. A force is a push or a pull that makes things move or stop.

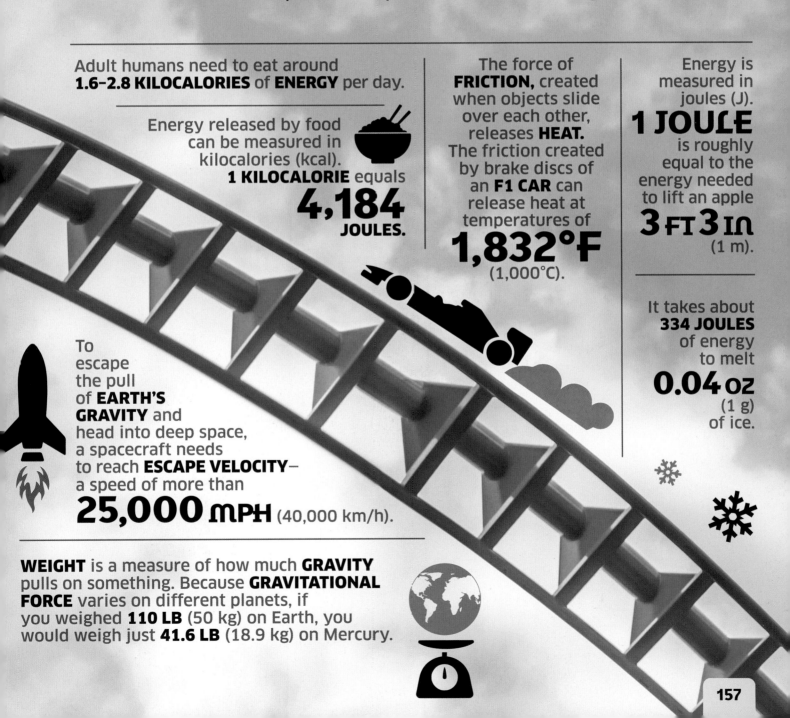

Adult humans need to eat around **1.6–2.8 KILOCALORIES** of **ENERGY** per day.

Energy released by food can be measured in kilocalories (kcal). **1 KILOCALORIE** equals **4,184 JOULES.**

To escape the pull of **EARTH'S GRAVITY** and head into deep space, a spacecraft needs to reach **ESCAPE VELOCITY**— a speed of more than **25,000 MPH** (40,000 km/h).

WEIGHT is a measure of how much **GRAVITY** pulls on something. Because **GRAVITATIONAL FORCE** varies on different planets, if you weighed **110 LB** (50 kg) on Earth, you would weigh just **41.6 LB** (18.9 kg) on Mercury.

The force of **FRICTION,** created when objects slide over each other, releases **HEAT.** The friction created by brake discs of an **F1 CAR** can release heat at temperatures of **1,832°F** (1,000°C).

Energy is measured in joules (J). **1 JOULE** is roughly equal to the energy needed to lift an apple **3 FT 3 IN** (1 m).

It takes about **334 JOULES** of energy to melt **0.04 OZ** (1 g) of ice.

SPARKS from some **HANDHELD FIREWORK SPARKLERS** can be as hot as **3,000°F** (1,600°C), which is higher than the **MELTING POINT OF IRON.**

In **1905, 11-YEAR-OLD** American boy **FRANK EPPERSON** left his **SOFT DRINK** containing a stirring stick outside overnight and **ACCIDENTALLY INVENTED THE** "popsicle."

880°F (471°C) is the average temperature of **VENUS,** the **HOTTEST PLANET** in the solar system.

In **YAKUTSK, RUSSIA,** schools are shut down for grades 1–5 when the **TEMPERATURE** hits **–49°F** (–45°C). The **OLDER STUDENTS** continue to attend school till the temperature falls below **–58°F** (–50°C).

HUMAN BODY TEMPERATURE is about **98.6°F** (37°C). That's just **8°F** (5°C) **HIGHER** than the typical *melting point of chocolate.*

The temperature of the **SUN'S SURFACE** is about **9,940°F** (5,500°C)– **2,700 TIMES COOLER** than its **CORE.**

–128.6°F (–89.2°C)–recorded at Vostok Station, **ANTARCTICA,** in 1983–is the **coldest temperature** ever measured at ground level.

Japanese macaques bathe in **104°F** (41°C) **HOT SPRINGS** in the **SNOWY** Joshinestsu National Park, Japan.

The energy of
HOT AND COLD

When the particles (atoms or molecules) in an object move, they emit heat energy. The faster they move, the hotter they are. An object's temperature is a measure of how fast its particles are moving.

355°F

(180°C) is the **TEMPERATURE** at which popcorn kernels **POP.**

The **HOTTEST TEMPERATURE** ever created on Earth was

9.9 TRILLION°F

(5.5 trillion °C), in 2012, inside the **LARGE HADRON COLLIDER**– a particle accelerator in Switzerland–that's

360,000 TIMES HOTTER

than the Sun's core.

TEMPERATURE is commonly measured using

3

scales: Celsius (**°C**), Fahrenheit (**°F**), and Kelvin (**K**).

ALASKAN WOOD FROGS freeze up to

60%

of their body to survive the **HARSH ALASKA WINTERS,** where temperatures drop from

16°F (-9°C) to
0°F (-18°C).

0 K

(Kelvin) or
-459.67°F

(-273.15°C) is known as

ABSOLUTE ZERO.

Nothing can get colder than this.

Water boils at
212°F (100°C) and freezes at
32°F (0°C). It is the **ONLY SUBSTANCE ON EARTH** to exist in all **3 STATES OF MATTER** (solid, liquid, and gas) in the **NATURAL TEMPERATURE RANGES** found on Earth.

The **EIFFEL TOWER** can grow up to

6 IN

(15 cm) taller on the hottest days, as the **IRON** used in the structure **EXPANDS** with rising temperatures.

The biggest-ever **ICE CREAM SUNDAE**–made in 1988 in Alberta, Canada–weighed
27.46 TONS.

1 lightning bolt contains enough electricity to boil water for **50,000** hot drinks.

In **1882,** American inventor **EDWARD H JOHNSON** hand-wired **80** red, blue, and white light bulbs together to create the **VERY FIRST ELECTRIC CHRISTMAS TREE LIGHTS.**

The temperature of a **100-WATT** incandescent light bulb filament is about **2,540°C** (4,600°F).

A **SINGLE SPIN** of the **80-M-** (262-ft-) long blades of a **VESTAS V164** wind turbine generates enough electricity to power a typical UK home for **29 HOURS.**

A **50-WATT** light bulb switched on for **20 HOURS** uses **1 KILOWATT HOUR** (kWh) of electricity.

ELECTRIC EELS can generate **800 volts** of electricity to **ELECTROCUTE** other fish.

In 2019, **12 COUNTRIES** generated at least **25%** of their electricity from **NUCLEAR POWER.**

Generating
ELECTRICITY

The modern world is powered by electricity, which can be converted into heat, light, or sound. It is generated using different sources of energy such as coal, gas, solar, wind, or water.

For a **WIND TURBINE** to produce electricity, the wind must blow at a minimum speed of **12 KM/H** (7 mph).

In 1881, London's **SAVOY THEATRE** became the **FIRST PUBLIC BUILDING** to be lit by electric lighting using some **1,200** of British inventor Joseph Swan's **INCANDESCENT** light bulbs.

The **UNITED STATES** used **13 TIMES** more electricity in **2019** than it did in **1950**.

Compact fluorescent lamps use **60–80% LESS ELECTRICITY THAN** incandescent light bulbs.

About **440 NUCLEAR POWER STATIONS** around the globe produce about **10%** of the world's electricity.

In 2020, **WIND** and **SOLAR ENERGY** generated **9.1%** of electricity globally.

In 2020, **35.1%** of all electricity globally was produced by **BURNING COAL** in power stations.

770 million people **DID NOT HAVE ACCESS** to electricity in 2019.

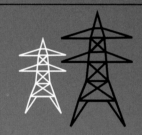

One of the world's **TALLEST ELECTRICITY PYLONS,** in China's Zhejiang Province, stands **370 m** (1,213 ft) tall.

A **2.5-MEGAWATT WIND TURBINE** can generate enough electricity to power **1,400** homes.

Everyday MATERIALS

We rely on a large number of materials to build our world. From giant buildings made of concrete, steel, and glass that dominate city skylines to garments made of cotton and silk, we use materials every day.

It typically takes

200 YEARS
for a **PLASTIC STRAW** and

450 YEARS
for a **PLASTIC BOTTLE** to biodegrade (break down in the environment).

The most heat-resistant material ever created is **HAFNIUM CARBONITRIDE.** Its **MELTING POINT** is more than **7,034°F** (3,890°C).

GLASS is made by **MELTING SAND,** along with some other ingredients, at temperatures of about

1,562°F
(850°C).

CELLULOID, a type of plastic, was invented by American inventor **JOHN WESLEY HYATT.** It qualified him for a

$10,000
prize offered for a material that could **REPLACE ANIMAL IVORY** in the production of **BILLIARD BALLS.**

In the **EUROPEAN UNION,** around

76%
of all glass packaging, such as jars and bottles, are **RECYCLED.**

Some forms of **SYNTHETIC RUBBER** can stretch to

100 TIMES
their original length.

Natural rubber
comes from the *Hevea Brasiliensis* tree. Each tree can produce up to **19 LB** (8.5 kg) **OF RUBBER PER YEAR.**

Recycling

25
small **PLASTIC DRINKS BOTTLES** can produce enough fiber to make a **FLEECE JACKET.**

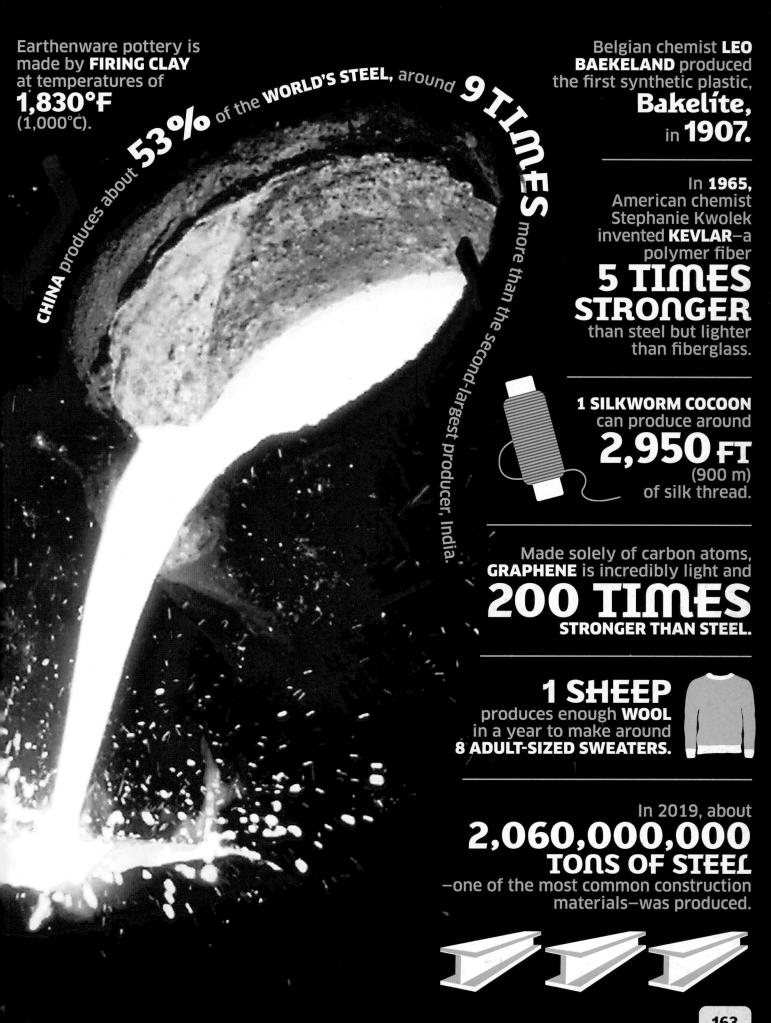

Earthenware pottery is made by **FIRING CLAY** at temperatures of **1,830°F** (1,000°C).

CHINA produces about **53%** of the **WORLD'S STEEL**, around **9 TIMES** more than the second-largest producer, India.

Belgian chemist **LEO BAEKELAND** produced the first synthetic plastic, **Bakelite**, in **1907**.

In **1965**, American chemist Stephanie Kwolek invented **KEVLAR**—a polymer fiber **5 TIMES STRONGER** than steel but lighter than fiberglass.

1 SILKWORM COCOON can produce around **2,950 FT** (900 m) of silk thread.

Made solely of carbon atoms, **GRAPHENE** is incredibly light and **200 TIMES STRONGER THAN STEEL.**

1 SHEEP produces enough **WOOL** in a year to make around **8 ADULT-SIZED SWEATERS.**

In 2019, about **2,060,000,000 TONS OF STEEL**—one of the most common construction materials—was produced.

Ingenious
INVENTIONS

Human curiosity has led to thousands of new objects, materials, and processes being created to make life easier and safer. Major inventions—from the wheel to the light bulb—have shaped our world.

British inventor James Dyson built **5,127 PROTOTYPES** before perfecting his first **CYCLONIC VACUUM CLEANER** in **1983.**

American **WALTER HUNT** invented the **SAFETY PIN** in **1849** and sold his patent for just **$400.**

American inventor Thomas Edison's 1879 **INCANDESCENT LIGHT BULB** lasted **13½ hours.**

The **FIRST WHEELS,** invented around **3500 BCE,** were used for **POTTERY MAKING.** They were not used for **TRANSPORTATION** until **300 YEARS LATER.**

In the 1800s, British chemist **HUMPHRY DAVY** invented the **ARC LAMP**—the **FIRST ELECTRIC LIGHT**—which created an **ARC OF ELECTRICITY** between **2 charcoal rods.**

In 2019, the **EUROPEAN PATENT OFFICE** received **181,000 patent applications** for new inventions.

...not invented until **48 years** later.

The **TIN CAN** was invented in 1810, but the **FIRST PURPOSE-BUILT CAN OPENER** was

A crowd of **130,000** watched the **FIRST hot-air balloon** flight in **1783**. On board were a sheep, a rooster, and a duck.

Thomas Edison owned **',093** US invention patents.

More than **100 billion ballpoint pens** have been sold since their invention in **1938**.

67 cents was the cost of the first ever **BARCODE-SCANNED ITEM**—a pack of chewing gum—in **1974**.

REFRIGERATORS became common household appliances in **1927.**

German watchmaker **STEPHAN FARFFLER,** who had broken his back as a child, built the **FIRST SELF-PROPELLED WHEELCHAIR** in **1655** at the age of **22**

In **1885,** American inventor **SARAH GOODE** became the **FIRST BLACK WOMAN** to gain a patent, for a **SPACE-SAVING BED** that folded into a **WRITING DESK.**

The first **MECHANICAL ALARM CLOCK** was invented by American Levi Hutchins in **1787**. It was nonadjustable and would go off at **4 AM EVERY DAY.**

American **GEORGE NISSEN** invented the first prototype **TRAMPOLINE** in 1930, when he was just **16**.

Super
STRUCTURES

Throughout history, humans have built countless cool constructions–from mathematically precise pyramids and fairytale castles to soaring skyscrapers.

By the 1990s, the **LEANING TOWER OF PISA**, Italy, was tilted at an angle of

5.5
DEGREES. Work to stabilize it reduced the tilt to **4 DEGREES.**

The **BURJ KHALIFA** in Dubai is the world's tallest building at

2,719 FT
(828.9 m) and has

160
FLOORS.

The **BUDDHA STATUE** in Leshan, China, is **71 M** (233 ft) **HIGH** and is

CARVED INTO A CLIFF FACE.

$1.5 million
WORTH OF COINS are thrown in the **TREVI FOUNTAIN** in Rome, Italy, **EVERY YEAR.**

2,194
SECTIONS OF CONCRETE. make up the roof of the **SYDNEY OPERA HOUSE.**

There are around **1,000 GIANT STATUES**–called *moai*–on the Polynesian island of **RAPA NUI.**

2.3 MILLION STONE BLOCKS were used to make the GREAT PYRAMID.

The Eiffel Tower

in Paris, France, is made of **18,000 iron pieces** held together with **2.5 million metal rivets.**

410,000 tons of **GRANITE** were blasted from the **Black Hills** in 1927 to create **MOUNT RUSHMORE** and carve the faces of **4 US PRESIDENTS.**

Around **18 MILLION BRICKS** and **475,000 TILES** were used to build the 17th-century **SHAH MOSQUE** in Isfahan, Iran.

The **GREAT PYRAMID** is the biggest and oldest of the **3 large pyramids** in GIZA, EGYPT.

The Statue of Liberty

in New York is **151 FT tall** (46 m). The torch, which symbolizes freedom, weighs **3,500 LB** (1,600 kg).

It took **8 years** to build **TOWER BRIDGE** in London. It has been open **SINCE 1894.**

ANGKOR WAT

is one of the **LARGEST TEMPLE** complexes **IN THE WORLD.** It covers an area of **0.6 SQ MILES** (1.6 sq km) at **SIEM REAP** in **Cambodia.**

80 arches formed the circular exterior of the **ROMAN COLOSSEUM.**

It took more than **20,000 WORKERS 22 YEARS** to build the **TAJ MAHAL** in Agra, India.

TOP 10
TALLEST BRIDGES

1 **MILLAU VIADUCT** • France
1,125 FT (343 m)

This 8,070-ft- (2,460-m-) long bridge in the valley of the Tarn River in France was opened in 2004. The road connects Montpellier in the southeast to the capital, Paris.

2 **RUSSKY BRIDGE** • Russia
1,053 FT (320.9 m)

This is the longest cable-stayed bridge in the world. It connects Russky Island and the port city of Vladivostok.

3 **SUTONG BRIDGE** • China
1,004 FT (306 m)

Travel time between the cities of Nantong and Shanghai was reduced by three hours with the opening of this bridge in 2008.

4 **AKASHI-KAIKYO BRIDGE** • Japan
979 FT (298.3 m)

Built with special features to withstand earthquakes, this is the world's longest and tallest suspension bridge.

5 **STONECUTTERS BRIDGE** • China
978 FT (298 m)

An international competition was held in 2000 to select the design for Hong Kong's Stonecutters Bridge.

6 **YI SUN-SIN BRIDGE** • South Korea
886 FT (270 m)

Named after a famous Korean admiral, the Yi Sun-sin Bridge connects the small island of Myodo-dong to the mainland.

7 **JINGYUE BRIDGE** • China
869 FT (265 m)

This bridge is one of more than 100 that cross China's wide Yangtze River.

8 **GREAT BELT EAST BRIDGE** • Denmark
833 FT (254 m)

At 833 ft (254 m) tall, the pylons of the Great Belt East Bridge are the highest points in Denmark.

9 **ZHONGXIAN HUYU EXPRESSWAY BRIDGE** • China
812 FT (247.5 m)

This cable-stayed bridge was constructed 440 ft (134 m) above the Yangtze River in 2009.

10 **JIUJIANG FUYIN EXPRESSWAY BRIDGE** • China
802 FT (244.3 m)

Around 220,500 tons of steel were used to build 20 miles (32.2 km) of cables for the Jiujiang Fuyin Expressway Bridge.

Wheeled VEHICLES

From cars, trucks, buses, and motorbikes to bicycles and electric scooters, wheeled vehicles rule the road. More than two billion of them travel on roads and bike trails around the world.

The **BROMPTON FOLDING BICYCLE** is built using more than

1,200 different parts.

The longest stretch limousine, AMERICAN DREAM, measured **100 FT (30.5 m)** long and had **26 WHEELS.**

Some **MOUNTAIN BICYCLES** have more than **40 gears.**

THE WORLD'S **LARGEST BUS,** Volvo Gran Artic, measures **98 FT (30 m) LONG** and can carry

300 passengers.

Lightweight bicycle **AX-LIGHTNESS VIAL EVO ULTRA** weighs only **9.7 LB** (4.4 kg)—less than some cats.

Pulled by **4 horses,** ROMAN CHARIOTS could race at speeds of **31 MPH** (50 km/h).

Far from being a new invention, **ELECTRIC CARS** had set **6 world LAND-SPEED RECORDS** by 1902.

The **BIG FRONT WHEEL** of some **PENNY FARTHING** bicycles have a diameter of **5 FT** (1.5 m).

A 2010 **TRAFFIC JAM IN CHINA** stretched for more than **62 MILES** (100 km)—one of the longest ever recorded—and lasted for **12 DAYS**.

More than **100 million** units of **HONDA'S SUPER CUB SCOOTERS** have been sold, making it **ONE OF THE BEST-SELLING MOTOR VEHICLES** in the world.

The world's first speeding ticket was issued to British citizen Walter Arnold in **1896** for driving at **8 MPH** (13 km/h).

The **TOYOTA COROLLA** is the world's best-selling car with around **48 million** sold in more than **150 COUNTRIES** since its launch in **1966**.

About **92.8 MILLION** motor vehicles were produced **WORLDWIDE IN 2019**.

The **LONGEST ROAD TRAIN** recorded was **4,836 FT** (1,474.3 m) long. It was made up of a **MACK TITAN TRUCK** towing **113 trailers**.

KAWASAKI NINJA H2R is the **FASTEST** street-legal motorbike in the world, with a record speed of **259 MPH** (400 km/h) in **26 SECONDS**.

The custom-built race truck that generate **36,000** **Shockwave horsepower** is fitted with **3 aircraft jet engines** and give it a top speed of **376 MPH** (605 km/h).

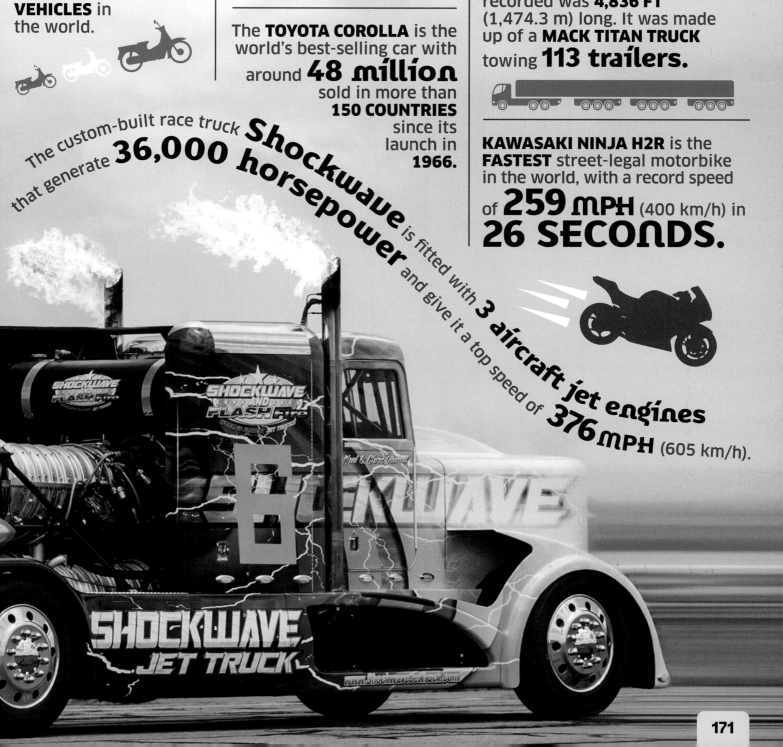

SHOCKWAVE JET TRUCK

On the
WATER

Since the first dugout canoes and rafts made more than 10,000 years ago, ships and boats have become a vital part of our world. Today, thousands of giant tankers and millions of fishing and leisure boats sail the oceans and seas.

With a **TOP SPEED** of
67 MPH
(107.6kph), *Francisco* is the world's
FASTEST FERRY
and can carry up to **150** cars and **1,024** passengers.

EARLY BATTLE CANOES built by people in Fiji were about **100 FT** (30 m) long and could hold around
200 WARRIORS.

The **OLDEST-KNOWN BOAT** is a **10-FT-** (3-m-) long **PESSE CANOE** that is more than
10,000 years old.

The *VESTAS SAILROCKET 2* is the world's **FASTEST SAILING BOAT,** with a top speed of
75.3 MPH (121.2 km/h).

The **WORLD'S LONGEST SUBMARINE,** the *Belgorod,* is about
11 TIMES
longer than the first **MODERN** submarine, the USS *Holland* (SS-1).

The **SWEDISH WARSHIP VASA** was launched in **1628**. It sank **20 MINUTES** after setting sail, but its wreck was only recovered
333 YEARS LATER.

About
4,600,000
vessels around the world are used for **FISHING.**

Between **1969** and **2004**, the *QUEEN ELIZABETH 2 CRUISE LINER* crossed the Atlantic Ocean a record
806 TIMES.

The **LARGEST CRUISE SHIP** in the world, *Symphony of the Seas,* is **1,188 FT** (362 m) long and can carry up to
6,680 passengers
and **2,200 crew members.**

A FORMULA 1 POWERBOAT can accelerate from
0–100 MPH
(0–160 km/h) in just
4 SECONDS.

The aircraft carrier USS *George Washington* weighs **97,000 TONS** and can hold up to **90 AIRCRAFT.**

Japanese World War II battleship **YAMATO** was armed with **9 GIANT GUNS** that could fire at targets **26 MILES** (42 km) away.

The **1,312-FT-** (400-m-) long *Ever Ace* can carry **23,992 SHIPPING CONTAINERS.** Every container can hold about **60 REFRIGERATORS** or **48,000 bananas.**

The **LONGEST-EVER SHIP** was the **1,504-FT-** (458.45-m-) long **SUPERTANKER** *Seawise Giant.*

MS TÛRANOR PLANETSOLAR is powered by **5,780 SQ FT** (537 sq m) of solar panels.

THE RMS *TITANIC* CRUISE LINER carried only **20 LIFEBOATS** for 2,240 passengers when it sank on its maiden voyage.

At **187 FT** (57 m) long and **73 FT** (22.3 m) wide, the Russian military *ZUBR* is the **largest-ever hovercraft** and can carry up to **500 TROOPS.**

In 1768, British explorer **JAMES COOK** made a famous **30,000-MILE** (48,000-km) trip **AROUND THE WORLD** in the **98-FT-** (30-m-) long HMS *Endeavour.*

In 1978, Australian Ken Warby set the **WORLD WATER-SPEED RECORD** of **317.59 MPH** (511.11 km/h) in *Spirit of Australia*, a **WOODEN SPEED BOAT** he built in his backyard.

The **OLDEST-SURVIVING STEAM LOCOMOTIVE**, *Puffing Billy* (completed in 1814), hauled coal for **48 YEARS.**

The world's **FIRST UNDERGROUND RAILWAY**, opened in **1863**, carried **38,000** passengers in wooden carriages through London.

The **NILGIRI MOUNTAIN RAILWAY TRAIN** in Tamil Nadu, India, travels at only **6 MPH** (10 km/h), taking **5 HOURS** to complete its steep uphill route.

New York City's **GRAND CENTRAL TERMINAL** has **44** train platforms—the most in the world.

16,627 FT (5,068 m) above sea level, **TANGGULA RAILWAY STATION** in China is the **HIGHEST** in the world.

At **35.5 MILES** (57.1 km) long, the **GOTTHARD BASE TUNNEL** under the Swiss Alps is the world's **LONGEST RAILWAY TUNNEL.**

The **LONGEST-EVER TRAIN** was made up of **682 wagons.**

In **1869, UNION PACIFIC NO. 119** transported railroad company vice president Thomas C. Durant to the **GOLDEN SPIKE CEREMONY,** celebrating the completion of the US **TRANSCONTINENTAL RAILROAD.**

The Trans-Siberian Express travels **5,772 MILES** (9,289 km) and crosses **8 TIME ZONES.**

LINE 2 of the Chongqing metro in China runs through the **6TH, 7TH,** and **8TH** floors of a **19-story apartment block.**

Terrific
TRAINS

Whether overground or underground, trains and railways keep millions of people on the move every day. Trains began linking the world long before cars and planes and today carry around 40 percent of the world's freight across land.

The world's **LONGEST STRAIGHT STRETCH** of railway track runs **297 MILES** (478 km) across **AUSTRALIA'S NULLARBOR PLAIN.**

In **1825,** British duo George and Robert Stephenson built **THE FIRST PUBLIC RAILWAY,** which ran for **27 MILES** (43 km).

375 MPH (603 km/h) is the **TOP SPEED** ever reached by a **MAGLEV TRAIN—** a record set in Japan in **2015.**

In **1934,** the *FLYING SCOTSMAN* became the **FIRST STEAM LOCOMOTIVE** to run at speeds of more than **100 MPH** (160 km/h).

25,000 volts of electricity run through the overhead lines powering **FRANCE'S TGV HIGH-SPEED TRAINS.**

At **4,481 FT** (1,366 m) long, Gorakhpur Junction train station in India has the world's **LONGEST RAILWAY PLATFORM.**

ARSENALNA on Ukraine's Kiev Metro is the world's **DEEPEST** train station, **346 FT** (105.5 m) below ground.

The United States has **182,412 MILES** (293,564 km) of **RAILWAY TRACKS.**

THE SHORTEST SCHEDULED FLIGHT LASTS 90 SECONDS and covers **1.7 MILES** (2.7 km) between the Scottish islands of Westray and Papa Westray.

There are **2 SHOWER SUITES** on board each Emirates A380 airliner.

13,422.7 MILES (21,601.7 km) was the distance covered by the **LONGEST NONSTOP COMMERCIAL FLIGHT**, traveling east from Hong Kong to London.

The Airbus A380, the **world's largest airliner**, can seat up to **853 PASSENGERS** in its 2 decks.

The pilots of **RED ARROWS** (The British Royal Air Force Aerobatic Team) fly their jet planes **AS CLOSE AS 4 FT** (1.2 m) from each other.

LZ 129 HINDENBURG, THE LARGEST AIRSHIP EVER BUILT, was **804 M** (245 ft) **LONG.** At its widest point, it was as tall as a **13-story building.**

6,000,000 PARTS are used to build a **BOEING 747-8 AIRLINER.**

In **1999,** an **MI-26 HELICOPTER** carried **A 23,000-YEAR-OLD FROZEN MAMMOTH** enclosed in a **26-ton ice block** from Siberia's tundra to a lab in Siberia.

In **1783,** the first **manned flight** was made on board the Montgolfier brothers' **HOT-AIR BALLOON** in Paris, France.

The **largest helicopter** ever produced, **RUSSIAN MIL MI-26,** has rotors **105 FT** (32 m) long.

In **1930,** nurse and pilot **ELLEN CHURCH** became the **THE FIRST AIR STEWARDESS,** flying on board a **BOEING AIR TRANSPORT** flight from California to Illinois.

Taking

FLIGHT

Since the first powered flight in 1903, air travel has quickly advanced. From passenger planes that travel the globe to stealthy military fighters, we rely on aircraft to get us to places fast!

12 SECONDS

was the duration of the **FIRST POWERED FLIGHT.** It was achieved by American duo the Wright Brothers in **1903** and covered a distance of

120 FT
(36.6 m).

In 2016, *SOLAR IMPULSE 2* became the first aircraft to **TRAVEL AROUND THE WORLD WITHOUT USING ANY LIQUID FUEL.** It was powered by **17,248 solar cells.**

110,500,000

PASSENGERS were handled in **2019** by the **WORLD'S BUSIEST AIRPORT,** Hartsfield-Jackson in Atlanta, GA.

The world's smallest

JET AIRCRAFT, the **BEDE BD-5J,** is just **12 FT 9 IN** (3.88 m) **LONG** and weighs **357.98 LB** (162.38 kg).

A **DC-10 AIR TANKER,** used in aerial firefighting, can drop **9,250 GALLONS** (35,000 litres) of water in just **8 SECONDS.**

TOP 10
FASTEST AIRCRAFT

X-15A-2 • First flight **1959** • Top speed **4,520 MPH** (7,274 km/h) • Length **50 FT** (15.2 m)

This US rocket-powered plane is not only the fastest aircraft ever recorded but also the highest-flying. In 1963, it reached the edge of space, 67 miles (107.8 km) above Earth's surface.

1

2 **LOCKHEED SR-71 BLACKBIRD** • First flight **1964**
Top speed **2,193.2 MPH** (3,529.6 km/h) • Length **107 FT 3 IN** (32.7 m)

Designed by the US as a spy plane to fly reconnaissance missions during the Cold War, the Blackbird was the fastest jet-powered aircraft.

3 **MIKOYAN MIG-25 FOXBAT** • First flight **1964**
Top speed **2,109.5 MPH** (3,395 km/h) • Length **78 FT 2 IN** (23.8 m)

The Soviet Union's Foxbat was the fastest combat jet, with two engines each capable of generating 24,700 lb (11,200 kg) of thrust.

4 **BELL X-2** • First flight **1955**
Top speed **2,094 MPH** (3,370 km/h) • Length **37 FT 10 IN** (11.5 m)

Nicknamed the "Starbuster," the Bell X-2 was a US research plane that was used to investigate the ways in which extremely high speeds affected aircraft.

5 **LOCKHEED YF-12** • First flight **1963**
Top speed **2070.1 MPH** (3,331.5 km/h) • Length **101 FT 8 IN** (31 m)

Long-range radar and infrared sensors were among some of the devices used by the stealthy Lockheed YF-12, an American prototype interceptor aircraft.

6 **XB-70A VALKYRIE** • First flight **1964**
Top speed **2,056 MPH** (3,308.8 km/h) • Length **185 FT** (56.4 m)

The US designed the thin, long-nosed Valkyrie to fly at high speed for thousands of miles, at a height of more than 70,000 ft (21,000 km).

7 **MIKOYAN MIG-31 FOXHOUND** • First flight **1975**
Top speed **1,874.7 MPH** (3,017 km/h) • Length **74 FT 5 IN** (22.7 m)

Designed to fly at lower altitudes than the Foxbat, the Foxhound still operates in Russia's Air Force today. More than 500 have been produced.

8 **MCDONNELL DOUGLAS F-15 EAGLE** • First flight **1972**
Top speed **1,864 MPH** (3,000 km/h) • Length **63 FT 8 IN** (19.4 m)

The American all-weather Eagle fighter has never been beaten in air-to-air combat, having racked up 101 victories.

9 **GENERAL DYNAMICS F-111 AARDVARK** • First flight **1964**
Top speed **1,649.7 MPH** (2,655 km/h) • Length **73 FT 6 IN** (22.4 m)

Developed in the US, strong turbofan engines lifted the Aardvark's 51,000-lb (23,300-kg) body off the ground.

10 **SUKHOI SU-27 FLANKER** • First flight **1977**
Top speed **1,553.4 MPH** (2,500 km/h) • Length **68 FT 11 IN** (21 m)

Made of tough titanium and aluminum alloys, the Soviet Flanker could also operate autonomously (control itself).

Going DIGITAL

No one owned a home computer until the 1970s or a smartphone until the 2000s. Progress has been rapid since. Shrinking electronic circuits onto tiny silicon chips has resulted in a digital revolution, with billions of phones, computers, tablets, and smart objects used everyday.

Around **200 UNITS** of the first Apple computer, the **Apple 1,** were made in **1976.** Each sold for **$666.66.**

In 1843, **28-YEAR-OLD** Ada Lovelace became the **WORLD'S FIRST PROGRAMMER** by writing step-by-step instructions for mathematician **CHARLES BABBAGE'S CALCULATING MACHINES.**

ENIAC, an early **PROGRAMMABLE** digital computer, weighed **30 tons** and filled a room measuring **50 FT** (15 m) in length and **30 FT** (9 m) in width.

A **MODERN VOLKSWAGEN CAR** is controlled by computer programs made up of more than **100 MILLION** lines of code.

Japanese Nintendo factory worker Gunpei Yokoi designed the **GAME BOY,** a portable game console, in **1989.** Around **118.7 MILLION** of these influential games consoles have been sold worldwide.

The first **PERSONAL COMPUTER,** the IBM 5150, had **16 KB** of memory. A modern **32 GB** smartphone has **2,000,000** times more.

More than **55 million tons** of old computers and other electrical items are **THROWN AWAY** each year. Only **ONE-FIFTH** of this **E-WASTE** ends up recycled.

Modern computers contain **100 million** tiny parts called transistors for each **0.002 SQ IN** (1 sq mm).

The computer aboard **APOLLO 11** had a **4 KB** RAM and **72 KB** memory and was less powerful than a modern **PHONE CHARGER.**

In 2020, Japan's **FUGAKU** super computer could make more than **415 QUADRILLION** calculations a second—making it **2.8 TIMES** faster than any other computer.

There were about **4.66 BILLION INTERNET USERS** in 2020, making up about **60%** of the world population.

The first supercomputer, **CRAY 1**, built in **1976**, was **8 FT 6 IN** (2.6 m) wide and contained **60 MILES** (96 km) of wires.

Many digital devices use a **GLOBAL POSITIONING SYSTEM** (GPS) of around **30 satellites** to pinpoint their location on Earth.

The **first mobile phone,** Motorola's DynaTAC 8000X, was first sold in **1984** for **$3,995.** It took **10 hours** to recharge its battery, which lasted for **30 MINUTES** of talk time.

14 MILLION VIRTUAL REALITY (VR) and **AUGMENTED REALITY** (AR) devices were sold worldwide in **2019.**

It took Swedish **MARKUS PERSSON** just **6 days** to create the **FIRST VERSION** of the computer game **MINECRAFT.**

By 2020, there were about **2.87 million** different **APPS** in the Google Play app store. The Apple app store had **1.96 MILLION.**

About **1,571 million** new **SMARTPHONES** were sold in the year **2020.**

A ROBOT-Rx dispenses **MORE THAN** **6,000 DOSES OF MEDICATION** in a day, saving **90%** of a pharmacist's time.

The Robobee X-Wing **FLYING ROBOT** is so small that **4** weigh as much as a single **paper clip.**

WasteShark, an **AQUATIC ROBOT,** can gather **1,100 LB** (500 kg) of plastic and other floating trash **IN A DAY.**

FIREFIGHTING ROBOT Colossus can withstand temperatures up to **1,652°F** (900°C).

Over **20 years,** Da Vinci Surgical System robots across the world have performed **MORE THAN** **5 MILLION OPERATIONS.**

Octinion's fruit-picking robot **RUBION** can harvest up to **794 LB** (360 kg) of strawberries a day– **7 TIMES MORE THAN A HUMAN.**

iCub, a 3-FT 4-IN- (1-m-) tall **HUMANOID ROBOT,** has **53** motors.

The word **ROBOT** was first used in **1920** in **KAREL ČAPEK'S** play *R.U.R (Rossum's Universal Robots).*

After travelling for **196 DAYS,** Saildrone became the **FIRST AUTONOMOUS ROBOT** to complete a journey around **ANTARCTICA.**

Versatile ROBOTS

Robots are clever machines that can move, sense, and sometimes even think on their own. They can achieve levels of strength and accuracy humans can only dream of. Today, millions of robots are at work in industry, research labs, and even the home.

In 2018, a **ZEPHYR S ROBOT** flew **NONSTOP** for a record-breaking **25 days, 23 hours,** and **57 minutes** without refueling.

A record-breaking **2,020 BASKETBALL SHOTS** were made in a row by **TOYOTA'S CUE3** robot in **2019.**

In 2009, **SCARLET KNIGHT** became the first **UNDERWATER ROBOT TO CROSS THE ATLANTIC OCEAN,** covering **4,600 MILES** (7,400 km) in **221 days.**

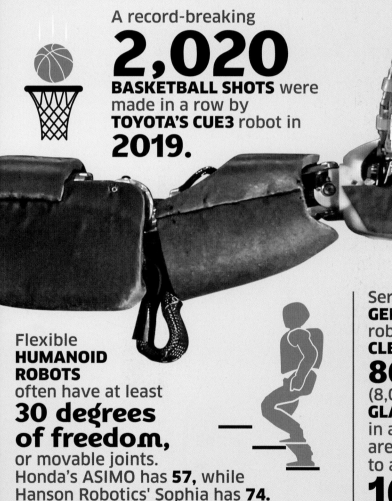

Flexible **HUMANOID ROBOTS** often have at least **30 degrees of freedom,** or movable joints. Honda's ASIMO has **57,** while Hanson Robotics' Sophia has **74.**

Serbot's **GEKKO** robot can **CLEAN** up to **86,000 SQ FT** (8,000 sq m) of **GLASS WINDOWS** in a day—an area equal to almost **16 BASKETBALL COURTS.**

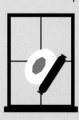

FANUC M-2000iA/2300, the world's **STRONGEST ROBOTIC ARM,** can lift objects weighing as much as **5,071 LB** (2,300 kg).

More than **1,300 SOFT, SEAL-LIKE ROBOTS** called Paro are used in Japan as a form of **PET THERAPY.**

ABB IRB 6640 robots perform **more than 4,000 welds** in just **90 SECONDS** to complete a **CAR BODY.**

GLOSSARY

Abdicate
To formally give up power and hand it over to someone else, such as when a monarch abdicates from the throne of a country.

Accelerate
When an object speeds up and goes faster.

Allies
A group of countries made up of Britain, France, the US, Russia, and others that fought against Germany and other countries in World War II.

Altitude
The height of something above the ground or above sea level.

Artillery
A part of an army made up of large guns or cannons.

Atmosphere
The layers of gas that surround a planet, held in place by the planet's gravity.

Atom
The smallest particle of a chemical element that can exist on its own.

Bacteria
Microscopic single-celled life-forms. Bacteria are the most abundant living things.

Battery
A store of chemicals in a case that when connected to a circuit supplies electricity.

Big Bang
The theory of how the universe formed out of a single point around 13.8 billion years ago.

Black hole
The remains of a star that has collapsed in on itself. Black holes have such strong gravity that they suck in objects around them.

Boiling point
The temperature at which a liquid can turn into a vapor or gas.

Byzantine Empire
An empire formed from the eastern half of the Roman Empire in 330 CE, which later expanded into more regions.

Caliphate
A state under Islamic rule, governed by a caliph.

Carnivore
A creature that gains its energy and nutrients totally or primarily through eating other creatures.

Cartilage
A tough flexible material that makes up the skeletons of some creatures, such as sharks.

Cell
A tiny unit of living matter. Cells are the building blocks of all living things.

Chlorophyll
A green chemical in plants that traps the energy from sunlight, which they use to make their food.

Circuit
A path around which an electric current can flow.

Circumference
The distance around the edge of a circular object.

Citadel
A stronghold or fortified building.

Climate
The general weather conditions a region experiences over a long period of time.

Colony
A country or area under the control of another nation.

Continent
One of Earth's seven large landmasses.

Currency
A system of money, such as coins, used in a country or region.

Density
The amount of matter contained in a given volume.

Diameter
The distance across the center of an object or shape, especially a circle.

DNA
A set of instructions for how a living thing will work, found inside its cells.

Element
A substance that is made up of just one type of atom.

Elevation
The height above a certain level, usually sea level.

Equator
The imaginary line around the middle of a planet, halfway between its north and south poles.

Erosion
The wearing away, usually of rock, by natural forces, such as flowing water.

Evaporation
When a liquid changes state to become a gas.

Evolution
The long-term process of change in living things, often taking place over millions of years.

Extinct
When a species of living thing dies out.

Extraterrestrial
Something from outside the Earth.

Filament
The thin strand of wire found in incandescent light bulbs that glows when electricity passes through it.

Force
A push or pull that makes an object move or stop.

Fossil
The preserved remains or an impression of a prehistoric animal or plant embedded in rock for thousands or millions of years.

Friction
The force that slows movement between two objects that rub together.

Fungi
A kingdom of living things, including mushrooms, that reproduce by forming tiny cells called spores and feed on decaying matter.

Galaxy
A grouping of millions or billions of stars all held together by gravity.

Galley
A type of ship used by the Romans.

Geyser
A hot spring that, at times, sends up a tall column of water and steam into the air.

Glands
Collections of cells in animal bodies that create and release substances, such as saliva and sweat.

Global Positioning System (GPS)
A navigation system using a series of orbiting satellites to give the accurate location of an object on Earth.

Gravity
The attracting force found throughout the universe that keeps planets in orbit and prevents objects on Earth from floating off into space.

Habitat
The natural environment where an animal lives.

Hectare
A measurement of area equal to 2.471 acres or 10,000 m².

Hibernate
To spend the winter or another cold period in a resting state, a little like a deep sleep.

Ichthyosaur
A type of prehistoric marine reptile that resembled a modern dolphin.

Import
To bring goods or services into a country.

Independence
The act of becoming free from the control of another person or country. A country that becomes independent is ruled by its own government.

Indigenous people
People who lived in an area before any settlers arrived.

Internet
A global network of computers that allows them to communicate and send information.

Laser
A device that emits a narrow, concentrated beam of single-color light.

Latitude
How far north or south of the equator something is.

Lava
Hot, molten rock from deep within Earth that erupts onto the surface from a volcano or other vent.

Light-year
The distance traveled by light through empty space in a year, approximately 5.9 trillion miles (9.5 trillion km).

Locomotive
A vehicle, propelled by steam, electric, or diesel engines, usually used to pull carriages or wagons

on a railway line.

Magnitude
The size or extent
of something.

Mammal
A type of animal
that is warm-blooded
with a backbone.
Mammals produce
milk to feed
their young.

Mass
The amount
of matter an
object contains.

Mecca
A city in Saudi
Arabia considered
the holiest city
in Islam, where
Muslims make
the annual Hajj
pilgrimage.

Megabytes (MB)
A measure of
computer memory
or capacity equal
to one million bytes
(a standard unit
of memory).

Melting point
The temperature
at which a solid
can melt and
become a liquid.

Migration
A long-distance,
often seasonal,
trip made by a
creature to find
food or to reach

breeding grounds.

Milligram
A unit of weight that
is one thousandth
of a gram.

Mineral
A solid substance
that occurs
naturally in Earth,
such as a single
element or mixture
of different elements.

Molecule
A group of elements
bonded together,
such as water
(made of the
elements hydrogen
and oxygen).

Mollusk
An animal with
a soft body and often
with a shell. Mollusks
include groups such
as snails, octopuses,
and clams.

Monolith
A single block of
stone, usually
shaped into a pillar
or monument.

Mosaic
A picture or
decorative design
made of small
colored pieces
of stone or tile.

Mummification
The process of
preserving a dead
body to prevent it

from decaying.

Nanometer
A measurement of
length equal to one
billionth of a meter.

Nerve
A bundle of fibers
formed from nerve
cells that carry
signals around
the body.

Network
A connection
between two or
more computers
that enables them
to communicate
with each other.

Newton (N)
A measure of
force equal to
0.225 pounds.

Orbit
The path of one
object around
another more
massive object.

Ore
A rock that contains
pure metals.

Organ
A part of a body
made up of many
cells and responsible
for a specific body
function, such
as the stomach.

Organism
A living thing,
such as an animal,

plant, or fungus.

Pharaoh
A ruler of
ancient Egypt.

Photosynthesis
The process by
which plants make
food from water
and sunlight.

Phytoplankton
Microscopic
single-celled
organisms that
drift near the
surface of the
ocean and make
food from sunlight.

Plesiosaur
A type of prehistoric
marine reptile that
had four paddles, a
short tail, and often
a long neck.

Pollution
Waste products
that reach the air,
water, or land and
can damage the
environment or be
harmful to the health
of living things.

Prey
A creature that is
hunted and killed
for food by
another creature.

Prototype
The first version or
an example of an
object or machine,
often built to test out

an invention or idea.

Protozoa
A group of single-celled organisms bigger than bacteria. They usually eat other microscopic organisms.

Pterosaur
A prehistoric flying reptile.

Rain forest
Dense forests of trees and other plants that receive high rainfall.

Recycling
The process of converting waste materials into useful new materials and objects.

Renewable
Referring to a resource that cannot be used up. Renewable sources of energy include wind power and solar power.

Retina
A layer of light-sensitive cells found at the back of the eye.

Scavenger
An animal that feeds on the bodies of other animals after they have been killed.

Shell (military)
A hollow case filled with explosives that is fired from weapons, such as tanks and guns.

Shoal
A large group of fish swimming together.

Siege
A planned attack to capture a place by surrounding it and cutting off access to essential supplies.

Solar panel
A device that converts energy from sunlight into electricity.

Solar system
The planets, moons, dwarf planets, asteroids, dust, and other objects that orbit around our Sun.

Soviet
Something created or owned by the Soviet Union—a group of Russian-led countries in Eastern Europe that existed until 1991.

Spacewalk
Any activity taken outside a spacecraft by an astronaut, usually to repair or maintain equipment.

Species
A set of living things grouped together due to their similarity and their ability to breed with each other.

Sultan
Usually, the Islamic governor of a place.

Supernova
The destructive and explosive ending of a large star, which scatters its matter through space.

Synthetic
A material or substance that is made by people and does not occur in nature.

Tadpole
A young frog or toad before it is fully developed.

Thrust
The force that drives a powered aircraft or rocket forward, usually produced by an engine.

Ton
A measurement unit of weight equal to 2,000 lb (907 kg).

Toxin
A poisonous substance produced by some creatures.

Translucent
Something that lets some but not all light through.

Treaty
A formal agreement between countries or international organizations, often to bring conflicts to an end.

Tsunami
A huge wave caused by movements in Earth's crust, such as an earthquake.

UN
Short for United Nations, this international organization is tasked with helping to keep peace and stability and to assist the most vulnerable around the world.

Venom
A type of toxin that is secreted by creatures, such as some snakes.

Virus
A package of chemicals capable of reproducing by infecting the cells of living things.

Volume
The amount of space that a substance or object occupies.

INDEX

Page numbers in **bold** show the most information for the topic.

ACKNOWLEDGMENTS

The publisher would like to thank the following people for their help in the making of this book:
Elizabeth Wise for the index; Hazel Beynon for proofreading; Hazel Beynon, Michelle Crane, and Jenny Sich for additional editing; Sahrish Hadia for the authenticity review; Heather Wilcox for editing the US text; Steve Crozier for creative retouching; Simon Mumford for cartography and 3D design; Sarah Hopper for additional picture research; Giles Sparrow for checking the space chapter; John Farndon for checking the Earth chapter; Richard Dearden for checking the nature chapter; Philip Parker for checking the history chapter; Emily Wren and Rodger Bridgman for checking the science and technology chapter; and Flora Spens for additional fact-checking.